CACHE Level 2

**Certificate in Understanding
Behaviour that Challenges**

Understanding Challenging Behaviour

Assessment 1

By

Dr Pedro Ramalho and Mr Sean Flynn

**The Cache Level 2 Certificate in Understanding
Behaviour that Challenges is fundamental
and necessary to every part of the caring
profession from carer to care home manager to
mental healthcare professional, to progress their
careers and better understand their clients.**

Dr Pedro Ramalho wants you to know you can do this. It looks hard but it is not, it is easy, you only have to care. If you care for your client as you care for yourself, you will never be defeated in this profession, however little you think you know, for in truth if you care to such a level you are already one of the best carers in Britain today. Which is why you are here, as a carer, for it   is care that leads to the understanding of a patients challenging behaviour and from that understanding, that the behaviour can be improved, thus a patients quality of life is improved. When someone asks what you are doing you can reply that you are literally improving someone's life. A noble goal with a noble end. Care and the improvement of a patients life is the fundament of our profession. The eternal truth is that we are all humans…...being, and in trying just to be, all of us need care. That is why both you and I care, and your care is just as important, just as valid and just as necessary as my care. Let us care together!

Mr Flynn interprets Dr Ramalho's thoughts and wisdom to the best of his ability. In addition to being Dr Ramalho's legal magician, Mr Flynn agrees with Dr Ramalho's principles of care and the reaffirmation that we are all in a caring profession, no matter how humble our position our care matters and is important. It is our profession and we are all professionals. Which is why we wrote these books, to enable you to not only pass but dominate your profession, with care and hard work you too can achieve what Dr Ramalho has achieved, 800 out of 800 points from the Cache Level 2 Certificate in Understanding behaviour that Challenges . Yes it is possible, yes it is achievable, his work is in your hands and it is this very work that gained that perfect score. Do as he does and you will only get better and care more, about everybody, especially yourself! Enjoy!

CACHE Level 2

Certificate in Understanding Behaviour that Challenges

Assessment 1

Answer to question 1 A: Explain what is meant by the following terms: Behaviour that challenges.

Behaviour that challenges, are "behaviours that are culturally abnormal behaviours of such an intensity, frequency or duration that *the physical safety of the person or others is likely to be placed in jeopardy* or *behaviour which is likely to result in the person being denied access to ordinary community facilities*." (**Eric Emerson** Lancaster University '**Challenging Behaviour: Analysis and Intervention in People with Severe Intellectual Disabilities**' 1995).

To simplify '**Behaviour that challenges**' is behaviour covered by two broad points:

1)   Any behaviour that puts a person or anyone around them at **risk**. Therefore the physical safety of the person or others is likely to be placed in jeopardy.

2)   Any behaviour that leads to a **poorer quality of life** for a person and those around them. Which could lead to a person being denied access to ordinary community facilities.

Behaviour that puts a person or anyone around them at risk

Some examples of Behaviour that challenges through **risk**, whether to the patient themselves or others include *self injury*, *hurting others*, *being destructive*, *eating inedible objects*, *running away* and *lack of awareness of danger*. These are challenging behaviours that are easily identifiable as putting a patient or those around them at **risk**.

From my personal experience with over ten years within the challenging environment of professional patient care, I have come across all of these risk based '**Challenging Behaviours**'.

1   **Self injury**:   A patient began to rip the skin from her own leg.

This was challenging behaviour that needed to be addressed immediately since there was **a risk of the patient damaging themselves and putting their safety in jeopardy** through infection of their leg.

2   **Hurting others**:   A patient starts to throw chairs around the lounge in the company of
        others.

This was a risk because **other** people could be injured or **hurt** by a flying chair.

3   **Being destructive**:   A patient throws a chair through a window.

This behaviour puts the patient and others at risk and places their safety in jeopardy since it results in flying **broken** glass and a dangerous **broken** window.

4   **Eating inedible objects**:   A patient starts to **eat** paper and was stopped.

This was done because there was a risk the patient may choke thus putting their safety in jeopardy.

5   **Running away**:   A patient **ran away** through the front door and was stopped.

This was because their was a risk the patient could collide with others or run out into the road and get run over thus putting his safety in jeopardy.

6   **Lack of awareness of danger**:   The same patient who ran away was heading for a main road.

The patient who ran away towards the road was **unaware of the danger** the road represented thus had to be stopped, as there was a risk he could be run over and put his safety in jeopardy.

These behaviours can clearly be classed as behaviours which put the physical safety of the patient or others in immediate **jeopardy** as per Emerson, or to put simply, place the patient or others within immediate **risk**.

Although other challenging behaviours such as **inappropriate undressing in public**, **spitting**, **stealing**, **verbal abuse**, **inappropriate sexualized behaviours**, **withdrawal**, **smearing**, **repetitive rocking**, **echolalia,** or as it is more commonly known as repetition of speech (echolalia from the word echo), are classed as challenging behaviours which are likely to result in a patient being **denied access to ordinary community facilities** as per **Emerson** since they lead the patient or others to have a poorer quality of life. Which is why you are here as a carer, for it is care that leads to the understanding of a patients challenging behaviour and from that understanding that the behaviour can be improved thus a patients quality of life is improved. When someone asks what you are doing you can reply that you are literally improving someone's life. A noble goal with a noble end. Care and the improvement of a patients life is the funderment of our profession.

Behaviour's which is likely to result in the person being denied access to ordinary community facilities and pose a risk to themselves or others.

Several of the challenging behaviours cross **Emerson's** dividing line between **risk** and **quality of life**, or as he says **immediate jeopardy** and **the denial of ordinary community facilities**. As they are challenging behaviours which can contain both risk to the patient or others and contribute to the patient or others a poorer quality of life usually through a denial of ordinary community facilities which results from such behaviour.

1   **Spitting**:   A patient spat in the face of another patient

4

This held the risk of infection, disease, etc, and contributed to the patients having a poorer quality of life through experiencing such an event. Should such behaviour be allowed to continue one of the patients would have been denied access to ordinary community facilities.

2   **Verbal abuse**:   A patient shouted verbal abuse at another patient who promptly had a   heart attack.

Usually verbal abuse is a challenging behaviour that is detrimental to the quality of life for the recipient of it, which leads to a denial of access to ordinary community facilities. However in certain cases verbal abuse can cause the physical safety of a person to placed in jeopardy.

3   **Inappropriate sexualised behaviours**:   A patient was inappropriately kissing another patient with such vigour that there was a high possibility of a fall putting both patients at risk.

Unfortunately inappropriate sexualised behaviours covers a broad church in relation to Emerson, covering the physical safety of the patient and others around them, and more commonly and intensely, leads to a patient being denied access to community facilities as well as contributing to a poorer quality of life.

4   **Withdrawal**:   A new patient was admitted who was completely withdrawn. He did not speak or move, but with patient tender care the patient became less withdrawn and more communicative thus leading to his successful treatment.

As can obviously be seen although withdrawal leads to a poorer quality of life for the patient and relations around them through a **lack of communication.** Certain cases of withdrawal lead to the physical safety of the patient being placed in jeopardy as in this case. Since successful treatment could not continue while the patient was in his withdrawn state.

5 **Smearing**: A patient started to smearing his own faeces on a wall in the dining area.

Although smearing is usually something that is detrimental to the quality of life of the patient and those around them by being messy, there are cases such as the above that lead to risk to physical safety. In this instance both the patient and those around him were placed in physical jeopardy from infection caused by poor hygiene.

Behaviour which is likely to result in the person being denied access to ordinary community facilities

1 **Inappropriate undressing in public**: A patient started to take his own clothes off in front of everyone in the dining room.

Although the physical safety of the person or others was unlikely to be placed in jeopardy, such challenging behaviour is likely to result in the person being **denied access to ordinary community facilities**.

2 **Repetitive rocking**: A patient was in front of the television rocking, and it was impossible to see anything on the television at that time by other patients in the lounge at the time.

Although such behaviour is easily dealt with in this case, it contributed to **a poorer quality of life** for the other patients who wished to watch the television and could result in the repetitive rocking patient being **denied access to ordinary community facilities** should his challenging behaviour continue.

8   **Echolalia**   The same patient above who was in front of the television was moved away from the television. After being moved he started to repeat the word "Kevin" loudly.

Again although there was no immediate danger of anyone's physical safety being placed in jeopardy from the patient repeatedly shouting "Kevin", **the quality of life** for himself and those around him was being reduced as nobody could hear the television. Also such behaviour can lead to him being **denied access to ordinary community facilities**.

Challenging Behaviour

The term '**Challenging Behaviour**' was introduced to replace a variety of terms which suggested that the problem was located within the person. The term 'challenging behaviour' was introduced to move away from this, by describing the behaviour as **challenging to services** ("this person presents us with a challenge in how to support him/her" as opposed to **blame** of the client "this person is being very difficult"). The emphasis was to encourage carers and professionals to find effective ways of understanding a person's behaviour and its underlying causes.

Answer to question **1 B**: Explain what is meant by the following terms: Positive behaviour

Positive behaviour

Positive behaviour is behaviour that is **socially acceptable** rather than **challenging**.

Although there are many positive behaviours most boil down to two general types. Positive behaviour is any behaviour that contributes to a patients **care** and/or a **patients quality of life** for themselves and everyone around them.

As with challenging behaviour I have also witnessed many examples of positive behaviour.

1   **Cooperation**:   A patient allowed me to dress their leg after I requested to do so.

The patients **cooperation** was a positive behaviour because it improved the patients quality of life and was clearly in the patients best interest.

2   **Agreement**:   I asked the patient if he would like to take his medication at that
          moment and he agreed.

This was positive behaviour because the patients **agreement** contributed to his care and quality of life.

3   **Showing affection**:   A patient gave comfort to another patient who was crying.

This behaviour was positive because the patient became happier and thus contributed to their quality of life.

4   **Making balanced criticisms**:   A patient made a balanced criticism that the television
was not working correctly.

This was positive because upon inspection of the TV set it was revealed that the aerial was loose, and after repair contributed to every-bodies quality of life.

5   **Understanding**:   The same patient who **agreed** to receive his medication informed me that he **understood** that the medication was necessary.

This was positive because the patients understanding improved the quality of his care.

6   **Listening to others**: A patient was shouting in the lounge where others were sat. One of them asked the shouting patient to stop shouting. The shouting patient **listened** to this request and duly stopped shouting.

This was positive because in showing consideration through listening he again improved the quality of his life and all those around him. Coupled of course that in listening he showed a very **socially acceptable** response.

Answer to question 2: Describe behaviours that might be perceived as challenging.

Verbal:

Common examples of verbal behaviours that may be perceived as challenging are:

1) **Offensive language**: Such as when a patient swears at another patient.

2) **Threats**: Such as when a patient threatens to hit another patient.

3) **Verbal abuse**: Such as when a patient begins to call another patient names.

4) **Screaming**: Such as when a patient begins to scream at another patient.

5) **Shouting**: Such as when a patient shouts over the television in the lounge.

6) **Echolalia**: Such as when dealing with a patient with autism.

These verbal behaviours may be perceived as challenging because the physical safety of the person or others is likely to be placed in jeopardy and/or the behaviour is likely to result in the person being denied access to ordinary community facilities.

Physical:

Common examples of physical behaviours that may be perceived as challenging are:

1)   **Hitting**:   Such as when a patient hits at another patient.

2)   **Biting**:   Such as when a patient bites another patient.

3)   **Scratching**:   Such as when a patient scratches another patient.

4)   **Pinching**:   Such as when a patient pinches another patient.

5)   **Hair pulling**:   Such as when a patient pulls another patients hair.

6)   **Throwing things**:   Such as when a patient throws a teacup at another patient.

7)   **Spitting**:   Such as when a patient spits at another patient.

These physical behaviours may be perceived as challenging because the physical safety of the person or others is likely to be placed in jeopardy and/or the behaviour is likely to result in the person being denied access to ordinary community facilities.

Non-verbal:

Common examples of Non-verbal behaviours that may be perceived as challenging are:

1)   **Pica (eating inedible items)**:   Such as when a patient eats paper.

2)   **Pacing**:   Such as when a patient continually walks up and down the stairs.

3)   **Cornering/Invading personal space**:   Such as when a patient forces another patient against there will onto a chair and then sitting   on them so they cannot leave.

4)   **Stealing**:   Such as when a patient steals another patients tea.

5)   **Rocking**:   Such as when a patient rocks in front of the TV in the common area.

6)   **Repetitive movements**:   Such as when a patient repeatedly taps on the table.

7)   **Damaging property**:   Such as when a patient damages his room door.

8)   **Withdrawal**:   Such as when a patient enters in a withdrawn state and will not
                answer questions.

These non-verbal behaviours may be perceived as challenging because the physical safety of the person or others is likely to be placed in jeopardy and/or the behaviour is likely to result in the person being denied access to ordinary community facilities.

Answer to question 3: Explain the difference between conflict and behaviour that challenges.

Conflict

'Conflict is a disagreement in which the parties involved perceive a threat to their own needs, interests or concerns. Disagreements are often the result of a misunderstanding and occur where opinions and points of view differ. Although conflict is often viewed as a negative thing, it is a normal part of life, for example in the workplace and in relationships.'

Behaviour that challenges

'Behaviour that challenges, are "behaviours that are culturally abnormal behaviours of such an intensity, frequency or duration that the physical safety of the person or others is likely to be placed in jeopardy or behaviour which is likely to result in the person being denied access to ordinary community facilities.'

The difference

As stated conflict is generally a disagreement, this indicates the parties **disagree**, this in turn indicates a level of **competency** and **control** between the parties. Behaviour that challenges do not need any element of disagreement since behaviour that challenges do not need any element of competency or control.

Secondly, even though a disagreement can can involve a threat to someone's needs, interests and concerns, this threat should not cause the risk of physical harm, as it would in behaviour that challenges.

Thirdly although conflict can involve misunderstanding and different points of view. Behaviour that challenges is not limited to this and can be easily recognized due to there intensity, frequency and duration. Going far beyond simple misunderstanding or a different point of view.

For example in the case of Martin (**Workbook 1 page 8**) we can see the differences between his **conflicts** and his challenging **behaviours**.

Martin thinks people are talking about him and making fun of him this is a **conflict** that needs to be resolved by working out the truth of the matter as to whether there is a threat to his needs, interests or concerns and gauging whether any misunderstanding is at hand.

Martin expresses **challenging behaviour** when he became withdrawn and isolated. This behaviour needs to be addressed. Next Martin expresses more **challenging behaviour** when he throws his meal tray at a group of colleagues. Again this **challenging behaviour** will need to be addressed through discussion with Martin.

Finally more **challenging behaviour** is exhibited when he runs out of the canteen and leaves work. Again this **challenging behaviour** would need to be addressed as Martin could be **excluded** from the canteen or even lose his job.

Answer to question **4**: **Explain the difference between aggression and assertive behaviour.**

There are a number of obvious differences between **aggressive behaviour** and **assertive behaviour**.
The main benchmark to aggressive behaviour is that it involves hostility to others and in some cases violence. Assertive behaviour does not. Aggressive behaviour is behaviour that shows no concern for the feelings or opinions of others. Assertive behaviour does show concern regarding the feelings of others and takes into account other peoples opinions. Aggressive behaviour is very selfish, inconsiderate and tries to blame others. Assertive behaviour is not as selfish as aggressive behaviour, it is more considerate of others and does not contain blame. Very much like the Japanese management style, assertive behaviour would not ask 'who is to blame' but rather 'what can we do about it'.

Aggressive behaviour is driven by anger, assertive behaviour is not. Assertive behaviour focuses on a problem, aggressive behaviour does not. Aggressive behaviour is unwilling to listen to others or consider anyone else's views, assertive behaviour is willing to listen to others and consider their views. Aggressive behaviour approaches a situation from their own viewpoint only. Assertive behaviour does not contain aggression and is willing to approach a problem from someone else's point of view not just their own. Aggressive behaviour can be verbal or physical attacks, assertive behaviour does not include any behaviour that attacks anyone either verbally or physically.

Certain traits are the hallmark of assertive behaviour. Honesty, confidence, understanding that it is wrong to violate the rights of others. Assertive behaviour can be **caring**, aggressive behaviour is devoid of this emotion. Assertive behaviour ables an individual to express themselves while allowing them to listen to others, and discuss opinions openly, aggressive behaviour allows for none of these things. An aggressive individual does not listen to others or discuss. It is far easier to build relationships with caring honest assertive behaviour than damaging aggressive behaviour.

Hallmarks of aggressive behaviour:

1   **Violent**

2   **Hostile**

3   **Little or no concern for others**

4   **Selfish**

5   **Blame others**

6   **Anger**

Hallmarks of assertive behaviour:

1   **Non violent**

2   **Non hostile**

3   **Concern for others**

4   **Unselfish**

5   **Cooperative**

6   **Calm and confident**

To conclude Aggression is defined as **an unplanned act of anger** while assertiveness is described as the ability to **appropriately expresses one's own wants and feelings**.

Answer to question **5**: **Describe how behaviour can be interpreted as a form of expression.**

All behaviour is a form of communication therefore all behaviour can be interpreted as a **form of expression**. However there are four basic types of behaviour that are most easily interpreted as a form of expression or communication. Hence their group title '**communication behaviour**'.

The four general types of communication behaviour are **aggressive**, **assertive**, **passive** and **passive-aggressive**. Please note that not all communication behaviour is challenging behaviour. Where as all challenging behaviour is

communication behaviour. Regardless of the reason for challenging behaviour it is sending us a message, it is **communicating**.

Communication Behaviours

1   Aggressive

Aggressive behaviour is defined as an **unplanned act of anger in which the aggressor intends to hurt someone or something**. Patients with aggressive behaviour are known as **aggressive communicators.**

Aggressive communicators typically create avoidable conflict by engaging in **personal attacks** and **put-downs**. Aggressive communicators create a **win-lose situation** and use **intimidation** to get their own needs met, often at the expense of others. Aggressive communicators typically feel a strong sense of **inadequacy**, have a lack of **empathy**, and believe the only way to get their needs met is through **power** and **control**. Aggressive communicators are usually **close minded**, are **poor listeners**, and tend to **monopolize** others.

Behaviours often seen during aggressive communication include: **putting others down, overpowering others, not showing appreciation, rushing others unnecessarily, ignoring others, not considering other's feelings, intimidating others**, and **speaking in a condescending manner**.
Aggressive behaviour can be verbal and non-verbal. Non-verbal behaviours exhibited during aggressive communication include: **frowning, critical glares, rigid posture, trying to stand over others**.

While engaging in this type of communications, individuals typically feel **anger, superiority**, **frustration**, and **impatience**. Aggressive communication often results in **counter aggression**, **alienation**, and **the creation of resistance or defiance**. Additionally, individuals on the receiving end of aggressive communication typically feel: **resentful**, **defensive**, **humiliated**, **hurt**, and/or **afraid**.

There are times when aggressive communication is pertinent, however. The aggressive communication style is essential during emergencies or when decisions have to be quickly made.

Encountering any of these aggressive behaviours such as **a patient putting another patient down**, **a patient attempting to overpower another patient**, **a patient not showing appreciation** or in other words being **rude**, **a patient rushing another patient unnecessarily**, **a patient who ignores another patient**, **a patient not considering others feelings**, **a patient intimidating others**, or **a patient speaking to another patient in a condescending manner**, are all examples of a patients **aggressive behaviour**. Since aggressive behaviour is **aggressive communication**, aggressive communication can be interpreted as an **expression** of aggression.

The art is to **listen** to the message a patients aggressive behaviour is telling you and rather than **reacting negatively** based on the aggressive behaviour, try to understand that a patients aggressive behaviour has a **reason**, it is a **communication**, and therefore an **expression**, find the reason for a patients aggressive behaviour and you can help the patient control his aggressive behaviour and therefore increase his care.

2   Assertive

Assertiveness is described as **the ability to appropriately expresses one's own wants and feelings**. Assertive communication is thought to be **the halfway point between passive communication and aggressive communication**. Assertive communication is based on the belief that each individual is responsible for his or her own problems; therefore they are responsible for directly communicating these problems to the other party involved. Assertive communication is a **direct form of communication** that **respects both the communicator's and the receiver's rights and opinions**. Assertive communication is direct without being argumentative. Engaging in assertive communication helps individuals **avoid conflict, maintain relationships, and usually ends in a win-win situation**.

Individuals who engage in assertive communication are **open to hearing the opinions of others**, **without criticizing their opinions**, and feel comfortable enough to express their own opinions as well. Assertive communicators generally have high self-esteem, as they have the confidence to effectively communicate with others without getting offended or being manipulative. While engaging in conversation, assertive communicators will **state limits and expectations**, **state observations without judgement**, **be an active listener**, and **check on others feelings**. Essential problem solving skills that assertive communicators acquire include **negotiations, confronting problems as soon as they arise**, and **not letting negative feelings build up**.

Behaviours that may be present when an individual is engaging in assertive communication include: **being open when expressing their thoughts and feelings**, **encouraging others to openly express their own opinions and feelings**, **listening to**

other's opinions and appropriately responding to them, **accepting responsibilities**, **being action-orientated**, **being able to admit mistakes**, **setting**

realistic goals, **maintaining self-control**, and **acting as an equal** to those whom are on the receiving end of the communication.

Individuals engaging in assertive communication convey **an open and receptive body language**, with upright posture and movements that are relaxed. Assertive communicators have a clear tone of voice and make appropriate eye contact.

Assertive communication has positive effects on both the communicator and the receiver. Some positive effects include: **the communicator feels connected to others**, **the communicator feels in control of their lives**, **the communicator is able to mature because they address and solve issues as they come up,** and creating **a respectful environment for others**.

3   Passive

Passive communication involves **not expressing one's own thoughts or feelings** and **putting their needs last in an attempt to keep others happy**. Passive communicators will **internalize their discomfort** in order **to avoid conflict** and **to be liked by others**. This communication style is typically exhibited when individuals **feel as if their needs do not matter** and that **if they voice their concerns they will be rejected**. Individuals who exhibit a predominately passive communication style usually have **low self-esteem** and may not be able **to effectively recognize their own needs**. They tend to trust others but they do not trust themselves.

There are many behavioural characteristics identified with this communication style. These behavioural characteristics include, but are not limited to: **actively avoiding confrontation, difficulty taking responsibilities** or **making decisions, agreeing with someone else's preferences, refusing compliments, sighing a lot, asking permission unnecessarily**. There are also many **non-verbal behaviours** that reflect **passive communication**. Typically, individuals engaging in a passive communication style have a **soft voice, speak hesitantly**, and **make themselves very small**. They also tend to **fidget and avoid eye contact**.

They typically possess feelings of **anxiety, depression, resentfulness, feelings of powerlessness**, and **confusion**. They feel anxious because their life seems to be out of their control and they acquire depressive feelings from a perceived sense of hopelessness. Passive communicators may become resentful because they feel as if their own needs are not being met and may become confused because they cannot identify their own feelings. People on the receiving end of passive communication typically feel **frustrated, guilty**, and **may discount the passive communicator for not knowing what they want**. While engaging in this type of communication, passive individuals typically feel **anxious** during the conversation and **hurt or angry** later.

Passive communicators tend to build **dependency relationships**, often do not know where they stand in situations, and will over-promote others, all resulting in **depletion of their self-esteem**. Passive communicators **do not regularly respond to hurtful situations, but instead let their discomfort build until they have an explosive outburst**. This outburst causes **shame** and **confusion**, leading the individual **back into a passive communication style**.

There are, however, numerous instances in which passive communication is necessary. A few situations may include: **when an issue is minor**, **when the problems caused by the conflict are worse than the actual conflict**, and when **emotions are running high**.

4   Passive-Aggressive

The Passive-Aggressive style incorporates aspects of both passive and aggressive communication styles. Individuals utilizing this style **appear passive**, **but act out their anger in indirect ways**. People who develop this style of communication usually feel **powerless**, **resentful**, and or **stuck**. A passive-aggressive individual exposes their anger through means of **procrastination**, **being exaggeratedly forgetful**, and or **being intentionally inefficient**, among other things.

There are many behavioural characteristics that are identified with this communication style. These behavioural characteristics include, but are not limited to: **sarcasm**, **being unreliable**, **frequent complaining**, **sulking**, **patronizing**, and **gossiping**. Non-verbal behaviours, such as posture or facial expression, can also reflect passive-aggressive communication.

Typically, individuals engaging in passive-aggressive communication have asymmetrical posture and display jerky or quick gestures. They may also have an innocent facial expression and act excessively friendly to conceal their anger or frustration. People on the receiving end of passive-aggressive communication are usually left confused, angry, and hurt.

They tend to be alienated from others because they elicit these unpleasant feelings. A passive-aggressive communication style does not address and properly deal with the pertinent issues or problems. This maladaptive problem-solving style keeps passive-aggressive communicators in a state of powerlessness, resulting in continued passive-aggression.

Examples of Passive-Aggressive Language/Behaviour include: **wistful statements**, **backhanded compliments**, **purposefully ignoring or saying nothing**, **leaving someone out**, **sabotaging someone**, and **muttering to oneself instead of confronting the issue**.

Answer to question 6: Explain how behaviour can be a symptom of something else.

Some challenging behaviour can be caused by **other factors**. In essence a challenging behaviour can be **the symptom of something else**. With challenging behaviour one of the first questions that should be asked is not just '**what**' the behaviour is but '**why**' is the behaviour happening.
Once you have found out '**why**' the challenging behaviour is happening, you can deal with the behaviour appropriately and correctly, to the benefit of the client.

Once you have found '**why**' a behaviour is happening, you can divine whether a challenging behaviour is a symptom of something else.

To clarify some challenging behaviours are not the problem itself but caused by something else.

Factors that may cause challenging behaviours

There are four main groups of factors that can cause challenging behaviour, **social factors**, **biological factors**, **psychological factors**, and **environmental factors**.

Social factors

Social factors that may cause challenging behaviour include:

1   An individual may be looking for **social interaction** and this may lead to challenging behaviour to get close to someone, or be noticed by them.

2   **Boredom** can often lead to challenging behaviour.

3   The individual may be **unaware of social norms and unexpected behaviour**.

4   An individual with challenging behaviour may be looking for some **control over their own   life and situation, wishing to make their own choices**. "**Give me liberty**, or **give me   death**!" (Patrick Henry march 23rd, 1775, St Johns church, Richmond, Virginia).

5   Others may be insensitive towards them and have a **lack of understanding** as to how to   interact with an individual with challenging behaviour.

Biological factors

1   **Pain** may lead to challenging behaviour as the individual is unable to explain how they are   feeling.

2   **Medication** can affect behaviour.

3   **Metabolic disturbances** such as Crohn's disease.

4   **Sensory stimulation**, such as hypo-sensitivity and hyper-sensitively. For example an   individual with autism who suffers from hypo-sensitivity.

5   **Confusion and forgetfulness.** A common occurrence with those suffering dementia.

Psychological factors

1   **Low or negative expectations**. If an individual with challenging behaviour feels that others   around them have low or even negative expectations of themselves this in itself could cause   or exasperate challenging behaviour.

2   **Loneliness**. Loneliness can lead to challenging behaviour.

3   **Social exclusion**. Individuals who feel socially excluded can try to gain attention by   displaying challenging behaviour.

Environmental factors

1   Trying to get something the individual with challenging behaviour wants, in other words some sort of **Desire**. For example physiological factors, such as **basic needs**, for example the desire for **food**, **drink** and **heat**, or the **desire for objects** can lead to challenging behaviour.

2   **The denial of desire**. Should an individual with challenging behaviour be denied what they want, for example being unable to join a social activity they may display challenging behaviour.

According to Rutledge S & James I (2007) in their book '**Staff's experiences of fearful situations when caring for people with dementia**', Rutledge found that 'challenging behaviour among people with dementia ranged from a prevalence rate of 30% to 60%. It was also found that 38% of incidents occurred when the individual was **denied something,** 20% involved a bath or shower situation and 17% involved verbal communication'.

3   **Noise and light**. A lack of, or overabundance of noise and/or light can cause challenging behaviour especially when dealing with individuals with **hyper-sensitivity** or **hypo-sensitivity**.

"**Nothing ever exists entirely alone; everything is in relation to everything else**" Siddhartha Gautama, Nepal 6 BC.

Answer to question **7: Describe possible reasons for behaviour that challenges.**

Once you have divined whether a challenging behaviour has a **cause**, or more simply a **reason**. The challenging behaviour can be dealt with.

For example:

Lack of ability to communicate

Some individuals with challenging behaviour have limited verbal skills or cannot speak at all. They may show or have challenging behaviour simply because they **cannot communicate** their desires and needs. For example an autistic individual becomes angry that a shop keeper does not understand their request for food.

Limited choices and control

Individuals with learning disabilities often have **limited choices** and **limited control over their own lives** which can lead to challenging behaviour. As the individual with challenging behaviour becomes frustrated at limited choices and a lack of control over their own lives. For example an elderly patient who is forced to eat a certain kind of diet because of their medication can become frustrated that food that they had previously is now denied them.

To define the cause of challenging behaviour there are eight basic questions to ask regarding the patients challenging behaviour.

1   **Is the individual with challenging behaviour hungry/thirsty/in pain/ill**?

2   **Is the individuals with challenging behaviour bored or frustrated**?

3   **Does the individual with challenging behaviour want to get away from a certain place,   or person**?

4   **Is the individual with challenging behaviour trying to avoid something**, for example a   person, or going to a certain place?

5   **Does the individual with challenging behaviour like the way the challenging behaviour   feels** for example rocking, or hand flapping?

6   **Is the individual with challenging behaviour scared/sad/anxious/angry**?

7   **Is the individual with challenging behaviour seeking attention**?

8   **Does the individual with challenging behaviour need or want something**?

There are many times a patient **cannot communicate**, through limited verbal skills, dementia or other factors.

1   **Lack of ability to communicate**.

This **lack of ability to communicate** means a patient can look for other ways to communicate and some of these other ways can be seen as challenging behaviour.

2   **Limited choices**.

Patients with dementia often have **limited choices**. This can cause challenging behaviour.

3   **Little control over their own lives**

Patients with dementia have **little control over their own lives** and this can cause challenging behaviour.

4   **Learned response**.

A patient may display challenging behaviour like damaging furniture as a way to influence what is happening to them, but it may be a **learned response** to get attention from nurses.

5   **Health issues**.

Patients with dementia often have **health issues** which leads to challenging behaviour such as a patient who is physically ill or in pain. Such health issues are possible reasons for behaviour that challenges.

6   **Life changes**.

Changes to healthy people's lives such as a death in the family, leaving home, changing school etc., may lead to challenging behaviour, since that is the case, it applies even more forcefully to individuals with challenging behaviour. For example dementia patients, such events can easily lead to challenging behaviour. From the beginning in fact a dementia patient faces a life change as their life and home is changed after the move in to the care home.

Answer to question **8**: **Explain how attitudes and lack of understanding can impact on individuals.**

In very recent times society has become much more progressive in its attitude to individuals with challenging behaviour. But many issues remain regarding common attitudes and lack of understanding of individuals with challenging behaviour.

Since Victorian times individuals with challenging behaviour were treated poorly and with great impact on their lives through a lack of understanding of their condition. Names such as 'Bedlam' still haunt the social conciseness even today.

Just like the Victorians many people today exhibit a negative attitude and a lack of understanding of individuals with challenging behaviour and the **reasons** for challenging behaviour.

Here are some common reasons and examples of peoples attitude to challenging behaviour and the impact it has on the lives of individuals with challenging behaviour.

1) Social Attitudes

Social attitudes form barriers to services such as leisure, transport, education, health care and other aspects of life such as social groups and employment.

Challenging behaviour is seen as **anti-social**. People with challenging behaviour go against the **social norm**. They can for example be withdrawn and have poor communication skills thus impacting negatively on the social norm.

Others may be loud, or seen as 'strange'. All of which can impact the individual with challenging behaviour negatively. Such discrimination affects those with challenging behaviour negatively and impacts on their lives on a daily basis.

2) Labels

Challenging behaviour has a tendency to have a **label**. The idea of such 'labels' is to inform people of the individuals challenging behaviour and better deal with it. Unfortunately since challenging behaviour is seen negatively and against the **social norm**, the labels have become negative and over time a general negative stereotype has entrenched itself into the social conscientiousness.

Once a person with challenging behaviour receive a diagnosis they are given title for their **condition** this can become a **label**.

For example: **ADHD**, **Dementia**, **Autism** etc. Such a label will impact individuals with challenging behaviours lives by **lowering their self-esteem** and **confidence** not through the title or 'label' of the condition itself but the lack of understanding and the **common negative attitude of the condition**. Such negative attitudes impacts individuals with challenging behaviour lives on many levels.

3)   Isolation

The individual and all those around them such as their carers and family can become **isolated**, either by negative social attitudes of others and/or misunderstanding of the condition/challenging behaviour. Society isolates the individual and their carers by staring at them, physically avoiding them, or simply point blank ignoring them. A common practice in Britain today. With such attitudes and lack of understanding it would not take long before the individual with challenging behaviour and those around them would cease to go out into such a socially hostile world and thus they would become isolated.

4)   Labelling

As discussed before when a person with challenging behaviour is given a diagnosis the individual is often **labelled** by that condition. In the social mind all such conditions are seen negatively thus a stereotype is born and discrimination flourishes this results in social stigma with name calling and ridicule being a natural result.

Such **negative attitudes** and **lack of understanding impacts the life of an individual** with challenging behaviour by degrading them. Placing them in a social tier way below the average, and making them feel at best inferior to their peers or at worst worthless. Which could easily result in the suicide of the individual with challenging behaviour.

This negative attitude and lack of understanding of the individual with challenging behaviour is not limited to ones peers but can also originate from people the individual trusts the most, their own family and friends. The individuals family and friends may not only ridicule them through name-calling as such when an autistic individual fails to get employment over a long period to the exasperation of their parents or names they are called by brothers and sisters.

There can also be other factors within the family circle that actively promotes a lack of understanding and negative attitude to challenging behaviour. For example **religious and cultural attitudes**, the challenging behaviour can be misunderstood and negative attitudes enforced by religious belief and cultural norms.

In some cases such religious belief and cultural attitudes can be extreme. Such as certain African states viewing mental illness as demonic activity with it's resultant negative social attitude based on a lack of understanding.

To summarize negative attitudes are the result of a lack of understanding. This lack of understanding impacts an individual negatively. The more we understand the better the world will be.

Answer to question **9**: **Describe the possible impacts and effects of behaviour that challenges upon the individual.**

A person with challenging behaviour **faces a negative impact upon their lives on a daily basis**. These impacts and their effects can be many and varied. Here are some common examples, but challenging behaviour can produce many impacts and effects upon the individual far beyond the scope of the examples below.

Social Exclusion

Challenging behaviour is often seen as **anti-social**. Therefore in most situations **anti-social people are excluded within a social setting or context**. Therefore an individual with challenging behaviour becomes **socially excluded**.

They will find it hard to socialise and make friends and this impacts their life negatively as an individual.

It is hard enough in this life to find good friends, how much more difficult for someone with challenging behaviour.

A good example of the impact and effects of behaviour on an individual would be the case of an individual with challenging behaviour becoming worse and worse over time and finding the root cause being that the individuals friends began socialising less with the individual with challenging behaviour until they was socially excluded and alone.

This would impact the life of the individual with challenging behaviour negatively.

In the above case, an increase in the understanding of the individual with challenging behaviour by their friends would have resulted in less challenging behaviour since their would be no social exclusion.

Injury

Individuals with challenging behaviour often injure themselves. Which is why it is so important to understand challenging behaviour. Individuals with challenging behaviour often **self-harm** to communicate to us of very serious problems, and such behaviour should be seen as very big red flag and a danger signal. For if such behaviour is left untreated death through self-injury can easily result.

Individuals with challenging behaviour can injure themselves by having a **high pain threshold**, and not notice hot objects such as a hot kettle, and burn their hands or pick up a knife from the wrong end and cut themselves. An individual with challenging behaviour can easily not realise that the world around them can harm them.

Infections from faeces and open wounds for example can be a complete mystery to an individual with challenging behaviour but its results will impact that individual and very negatively effect them.

To this end in extreme cases the individual with challenging behaviour could be **restrained** by mechanical restraints such as a straight jacket or protective devices. The dangers of injury to the individual with challenging behaviour in these cases are obvious and apparent, as in such cases there can be **tendon damage** and **dislocation of limbs** to the **demineralisation of the bones** and **muscular atrophy** due to the individual with challenging behaviour being placed in such confines for very long periods.

A practice that does not sit well with me, already rare hopefully with more understanding such cases will become unheard of.

Learning

Another very important impact upon an individual with challenging behaviour is their **learning**.

Challenging behaviour can effect and impact an individuals learning at all levels very negatively.

Not just in the classroom environment where challenging behaviour can lead to exclusion but depending on the behaviour in any setting or environment where the individual needs to learn something, within the family home, education between mother and son, within the workplace where the individual with challenging behaviour needs to learn the office procedures and practices, or simply being advised on the safest way to cross a road.

Challenging behaviour impacts and effects the individuals learning regardless of what is being learnt.

This in itself should be born seriously in mind and more emphasis should be placed on helping and understanding this principle. Individuals with challenging behaviour should be helped whenever necessary and to the fullest extent.

If an individual with challenging behaviour can learn, especially about themselves, they will understand themselves more. In that self-understanding they can help themselves more and thus continue to make a positive contribution to their own lives. Which in turn can reduce the impacts and effects of their challenging behaviour on themselves as individuals and all those around them.

For without learning we become barbarians.

Answer to Q10: Describe the possible impact and effects of behaviour that challenges on others.

An individual with challenging behaviour effects not only themselves but all those around them, and those effects impact their lives.

The greatest effects and impacts of an individual with challenging behaviour are felt upon themselves but serious consideration must be placed upon not only the individual with challenging behaviour but also those closet around them. Their family, carers, friends and loved ones. For as challenging behaviour effects and impacts on an individuals life it also has effects and impacts on others.

Those effects and impacts can and do put strain upon those around individuals with challenging behaviour in a variety of ways. Being able to spot those impacts enables these impacts to be reduced, relieving the strain and make it easier for those around an individual with challenging behaviour to cope, and thus improve the quality of life of not only those around an individual with challenging behaviour but the individual himself.

One has a **duty of care** not only regarding the individual themselves but with those around them. **We may be carers in word but we must be carers in deed**.

Let us look at some common examples of the impacts and effects of challenging behaviour.

1)   **Family and carers focused too much on the individual with challenging behaviour to the detriment of the family or carers own well-being.**

Parents, family, friends, carers and loved ones can be so focused upon the individual with challenging behaviour that they neglect their own needs and in extreme situations it can begin to affect their health.

2)   **The effects and impacts upon the relationship the individual with challenging behaviour has with others.**

Challenging behaviour impacts and affects all of an individual with challenging behaviour relationships. Those closest to the individual with challenging behaviour receive after the individual themselves the greatest impact, and most strain.

3)   **Those living with the individual with challenging behaviour.**

It is one thing to be eight hours a day at a job, it is another to be there twenty four hours, and that is what it is like for those that live with individuals with challenging behaviour.

Extra strain is placed upon those living with the individual with challenging behaviour from not only the challenging behaviour itself but all the strains that result from dealing with it for very long periods.

4)   **Individuals who self-harm or have toilet issues**.

The impact and effects on others by individuals with challenging behaviour of self-harm or toilet issues can be considerable.

The question would not be whether such challenging behaviour could cause impacts and effects upon others. It would be a question of such challenging behaviour will have impacts and effects upon others. The only question is how many impacts and how great will be the effects.

5)   **Older parents being carers which becomes more difficult and demanding with age**.

Time and tide wait for no man, and as the individual with challenging behaviour ages so do their carers. With age comes all of its burdens, diminished strength, diminished energy and the desire to live life a bit more slowly.

Yet the burden of caring for an individual with challenging behaviour gets no lighter with age.

In fact the reverse is true, the impacts and effects double as both the carer and individual with challenging behaviour age. The older they become the greater the impacts and effects.

6)   **Health Issues**

One would also add not only is the age of the carer of an individual with challenging behaviour a factor in possible impacts and effects of challenging behaviour on others but also health related issues.

Growing old makes caring for an individual with challenging behaviour hard but also the health of the carers themselves. If a carer has health problems this can be impacted by the individuals challenging behaviour and have effects.

Effects of challenging behaviour

Here are some examples of the effects of challenging behaviour.

1)   **Physical harm resulting from aggressive behaviour.**

Some challenging behaviour can manifest itself in some violent act which harms the carer, or loved one.

The impact and effects on others that would receive such harm merely one time let alone on a daily basis or in some cases hourly basis would be severe. Strain would be expected and the impacts and effects would range from the physical (pain) to the psychological (fear/shock) at the minimum.

It is a hard road to walk when dealing with individuals with challenging behaviour who would harm you.

2)   **Being excluded from social situations or unable to go out or spend time away from home**.

Caring for an individual with challenging behaviour can mean being excluded from social situations. From missing out on a night out because you have to stay in and care for an individual with challenging behaviour to not being invited to anything with anyone because nobody else can deal with the individual with challenging behaviour. This puts strain on the carer of an individual with challenging behaviour.

3)   **Tiredness due to constant demands of their caring role**.

A man has only so much strength. At some point the constant demands of care will begin to effect and impact the carer. Tiredness of a carer of an individual with challenging behaviour negatively effects and negatively impacts the lives of the carer and the very care they are trying to achieve.
The carer literally becomes too tired to care.

Tiredness itself brings a multitude of risks and multiplies the probability of accidents both to oneself and the person you are trying to care for.

Studies have shown that a lack of sleep for twenty four hours is the equivalent to trying to drive after a bottle and a half of scotch whisky. One can easily imagine the caring capability of a carer who had consumed such an amount of alcohol.

4)   **Financial issues if they have to give up work to be carers**.

This is arguably the greatest impact and effect on the behaviour of others. If a carer has to make a large financial sacrifice to care for the individual with challenging behaviour there will be guaranteed strain. Guaranteed impacts and effects. How long indeed would it be before the carer is unable to care due to financial problems. It could get financially worse before it gets better or never get financially better. When money goes out the window love goes out the door. The future of care becomes in jeopardy and the quality of the care from a carer under such strain will be affected.

5)   **Health issues due to stress and lack of concern with their own well-being**.

Stress caused by the impacts and effects of challenging behaviour and caring for an individual with challenging behaviour is common, and some carers do not know their own limits attempting to perform the impossible and damaging themselves in the process. Overstressing themselves and placing upon themselves the burden of care without taking advantage of support mechanisms and structures available to ease that burden of care. An overstressed carer can develop new health issues, lower the quality of care and reduce the capability of care.

6)   **Being judged by others**.

Since challenging behaviour is seen as anti-social and negative some cares feel as if society, friends, neighbours and family judge the carer for the display's of challenging behaviour. The mother is quickly judged on the behaviour of the child, so it is with the carer and the individual with challenging behaviour. You the carer are held responsible because it may be the individual with challenging behaviour cannot be held responsible because of their mental capacity. So if you are responsible you are to blame, it is suddenly your fault. Judgement by society is a common and harsh effect of dealing with an individual with challenging behaviour.

Negative Emotional Reactions to Challenging Behaviour and Staff Burnout

David Rose (Psychology Department, Dudley South Primary Care NHS Trust) in his 1995 collaborative work '**Negative emotional reactions to challenging behaviour and staff burnout**' found that "challenging behaviours such as self-harm, aggression, and damage to property are a major cause of stress to families and carers", and "significant positive correlations were found between negative emotional reactions to challenging behaviour and emotional exhaustion and depersonalization burnout". If faced with such challenging behaviours know there will be impacts and effects on others.

Answer to Q11: **Explain how behaviour that challenges may potentially impact own and others feelings and attitudes**.

Challenging behaviour is not only an issue in itself it also harbours the potential to impact and affect the feelings and attitudes of the individual with challenging behaviour and all those around them.

As Thufir Hawat (Dune) once said "The first step in avoiding the trap is knowing of its existence." Being aware of these potential impacts means that they can be dealt with correctly and quickly thus helping the individual with challenging behaviour and all those around them.

These potentials for impact on own and others feelings and attitudes are based on three factors who, how long and what.

Who

The who is who is the person who may be impacted by their own feelings and attitudes and/or the feelings and attitudes of those around them.

Is the '**who**' the individual with challenging behaviour themselves, or their carers, or family, their friends, their boss. Each person will have potential impacts and each persons attitudes and feelings will be different.

Like a stone falling into a pond, ripples are made and like a stone challenging behaviour impacts with the potential to affect a wide area around itself.

How Long

How long is the duration of time that the individual with challenging behaviour or others have been experiencing not only the challenging behaviour but the impact of the challenging behaviour on their own feelings and attitudes. Also how long could these potentials for impact last. Is it long term impacts and effects with displays of challenging behaviour over weeks, months or even years or short term impacts and effects with displays of challenging behaviour lasting hours or minutes.

The longer the impacts of challenging behaviour on an individual and others feelings and attitudes the harder the task of dealing with these impacts and the more potential there is for further impacts and effects on the feelings and attitudes of the individual with challenging behaviour and those around them.

What

What is not only 'what' is the challenging behaviour but 'what' are the potentials to impact the individual with challenging behaviour's feelings and attitudes and those around them.

'**What**' are the feelings and attitudes of the individual with challenging behaviour. Can these feelings and attitudes be improved. What has caused them to deteriorate, are there problems on the horizon, is there a potential that an individual with challenging behaviour's feelings and attitudes will change and be impacted for the worse.

What are the feelings and attitudes of the people around the individual with challenging behaviour. What are the potentials for these feelings and attitudes to be impacted by the challenging behaviour.

"What! My dear Watson! That is the key." (Sherlock Holmes)

Like Holmes people who deal with challenging behaviour become detectives, finding out the mystery from the clues. The what that lies behind the potential impacts on the individuals feelings and attitudes as well as all those around them not only in the short term but long term as well.

Here are some common examples of feelings that an individual or others may have when dealing with challenging behaviour:

1)   **The individual with challenging behaviour may feel frustrated and angry.**

The reason for this impact on their attitude and feelings may be because the individual with challenging behaviour cannot communicate effectively and therefore not have their needs met.

2)   **The individual with challenging behaviour may feel isolated.**

These feelings of isolation may stem from people around the individual with challenging behaviour avoiding them and not wishing to socialise with them, or accept them in their social group.

The potential of social isolation from challenging behaviour is high as evidenced by its frequency. It is very common that after a short amount of time an individual with challenging behaviour becomes socially isolated.

If this social isolation continues in the long term it can lead to intense feelings of loneliness and depression. No man is an island.

3) **The individual with challenging behaviour feels increased loneliness and depression that they may be made homeless by their family.**

Long term social isolation to the individual with challenging behaviour or those around them can lead to the loss of the family home and environment if the individual with challenging behaviour's carer or family can no longer cope with the challenging behaviour and its impacts and effects. Housing options may break down, carers leave, money becomes an issue. These impacts and effects can place the home environment of the individual with challenging behaviour in jeopardy and thus potentially impact the individual with challenging behaviour's feelings and attitudes and those around them.

Behaviour that challenges may potentially impact the individual with challenging behaviour and others attitudes and feelings in the short and long term.

Short term

1) **Fear**

People caring for individuals with challenging behaviour often feel frightened by the behaviour especially if it is violent or aggressive. Fear is an immediate emotion therefore it is an immediate potential for impact on the feelings and attitudes of the receiver of fear a well as all those around them.

Not only is the carer impacted by fear but also the individual with challenging behaviour as feelings of guilt and remorse can turn to depression, or the resultant social isolation could lead to further aggressive behaviour.

2)   **Dislike**

Others may dislike the individual due to their challenging behaviour and the effect it is having on themselves, the individual, the individuals family and the individuals social circle.

Dislike is another immediate potential impact on an individuals feelings and attitudes and others around them. The potential impact can be varied and wide ranging from simple discomfort resulting from the challenging behaviour or feeling awkward if you are the individual with challenging behaviour to violent hatred resulting from the challenging behaviour or violent self-loathing leading to self-harm and possible suicide.

Although dislike is a short term impact of challenging behaviour if left unresolved dislike can fester and give rise to more serious and long-term effects and problems.

3)   **Aggression**

Aggression is a very common and immediate potential impact on an individuals feelings and attitudes and others around them. An individual with challenging behaviour can become aggressive through being provoked by some behaviours that they are experiencing. Such as an individual with challenging behaviour becoming aggressive because their challenging behaviour causes them pain so they retaliate by becoming aggressive to the carer.

Aggression also causes the carer to become frightened which can impact the carers attitude and feelings of the individual with challenging behaviour. If an individual with challenging behaviour is or becomes aggressive the potential for impacts on the feelings and attitudes on themselves and others goes from possibility to probability. Aggressive behaviour is something that would need to be dealt with quickly, if left unresolved over time the potential for impacts and effects to the individual with challenging behaviour will escalate from probability to certainty.

Again asking the 'why' is that behaviour happening. As with cause and effect, the cause of the aggression begins by being unknown but the effect is obvious, your job as a carer is to make the cause obvious and to make the effects unknown.

4)   **Anger and upset**

If an individual with challenging behaviour becomes angry or upset there is a potential to impact the feelings and attitudes of those around them. An individual with challenging behaviour can become angry at not being able to communicate, for example not being understood while trying to buy a chocolate bar and begin getting angry and shouting, or upset over their challenging behaviour leading them to some sort of social exclusion like people not inviting the individual with challenging behaviour to a family get together.

This anger and upset can be easily misunderstood, being seen as a cause (they are angry) instead of an effect (why are they angry).

It is also very easy for other people around the individual with challenging behaviour to become angry and upset over the displays of challenging behaviour.

Many challenging behaviours can make individuals and others angry and upset. Dealing with challenging behaviour involving metabolic disturbances, dealing with an individual with challenging behaviour who has psychological issues ect.

If the individual with challenging behaviour is making those around themselves angry and upset then questions have to be asked quickly to resolve issues.

The potential impact to the feelings and attitude of the individual with challenging behaviour will be very likely, if those around the individual with challenging behaviour become angry and upset.

An angry carer is no carer at all, and as old Ben said "Anger leads to to the dark side".

Long Term

1)   Despair

Carers with little understanding of challenging behaviour may feel things are out of their control if their care appears to be having no effect on an individual with challenging behaviour.

When dealing with challenging behaviour one has to understand that Rome wasn't built in a day and some people do not understand Rome. Dealing with challenging behaviour can be a long process and the results of care can take a long time to show themselves and be of limited scope, depending on the challenging behaviour.

Despair at challenging behaviour both from the individual with challenging behaviour and their carers can result if either party believes they can no longer cope or they are having no effect on the challenging behaviour.

Both the individual with challenging behaviour and their carers must have their confidence boosted to avoid despair. To show that their care and hard work matters. They matter. That they are having a positive effect and although the behaviour is challenging that they have the capability to rise to its challenge and one day by the grace of God, master it!

2)   **Responsibility**

The individual with challenging behaviour or their carers may feel responsible for the impacts and effects of the challenging behaviour. This potential impact of responsibility for the challenging behaviour is a form of blame. The individual or others feel blame for the challenging behaviour and/or its effects.

They feel responsible in some way so feel they are the one to blame. Which is a very well established and long term western social norm. The impacts and effects of responsibility for the challenging behaviour by either the individual or those around them are exacerbated by this long term social norm, after all if its your fault you are to blame. In many cases this responsibility for challenging behaviour is misplaced.

The individual who has the challenging behaviour may not actually be responsible for it. A dementia patient cannot be held responsible for forgetting something. Likewise others around the individual with challenging behaviour most times cannot be held responsible for the challenging behaviour or its impacts and effects.

A mother is responsible for a son, but there are many things that a son does that are out of her control and she cannot be responsible for.

If a dementia patient cannot be held responsible for forgetting something, their carer cannot be held responsible for the patients forgetfulness since the carer is not responsible for the dementia.

Responsibility rests with authority. People feel responsible and so assign blame. If there is no authority there can be no responsibility. Many times the individual with challenging behaviour or others around them feel responsible and thus blame themselves. Yet with no control of the challenging behaviour or its impacts and effects the individual with challenging behaviour or those around them have no power, because they have no control and without the power to do something you gain the authority to do nothing. Without such authority you cannot be responsible.

If the individual with challenging behaviour or those around them did not author the challenging behaviour and its impacts and effects they cannot be held responsible for them.

Like the Japanese say "Look not to who is responsible but what can be done now!"

In such events of individual with challenging behaviour or others around them facing the potential impacts of challenging behaviour brought on from feeling responsible for that behaviour and it's impacts and effects when they are not responsible should be encouraged by the truth.

That they are not responsible for the challenging behaviour and its impacts and effects. They are not to blame. It's not their fault.

If they are not at fault then look not to who is to blame for there is no blame and look only to what can be done now. Throw off the burdens of the past my friend and Carpe Diem! Seize the day!

3)   **Shame**

If necessity is the mother of invention then shame is the brother of blame. Within society they go together hand in hand. Once you get the blame you receive the shame.

Shame is a very powerful impact of challenging behaviour both to the individual with challenging behaviour and those around them. The challenging behaviour and its impacts can cause shame to the individual with challenging behaviour and their carers within all levels of society from home environment, work environment, and the general environment.

For usually when an individual with challenging behaviour or those around them feel responsible for the challenging behaviour and its impacts and effects I.e. the blame. They then feel the shame. They are responsible therefore feel ashamed, even if they are not in fact responsible.

It is easy in this society to feel shame. Even people who have no challenging behaviour struggle. Shame is evident everywhere. Shame forces you to do many things, the correct clothes, the ever present competitive war between neighbours, draining demands of going out and looking good, the correct pub, the coolest club, the correct behaviour, the best image.

Get these social questions wrong and you will fall down the social ladder. You will feel ashamed, you will feel embarrassed. Because the demands are so high in modern society that the smallest mistake is revealed and mocked, leading to embarrassment which leads to shame and the acceptance of responsibility.

If the life of those without challenging behaviour is so hard within society, then individuals with challenging behaviour and those around them face a much more difficult task as almost all challenging behaviour is deemed as shameful in one way or another.

A dementia patient who forgets the name of the day can be mocked for being stupid thus feeling shame. A dementia patient who cannot remember the name of a close loved one can feel terrible shame at not knowing such an important fact.

Shame is a very common potential impact on an individual with challenging behaviour and others around them. Some individuals with challenging behaviour and others around them can feel shame because they feel they are not able to control the challenging behaviour of the individual, but since they cannot control the behaviour, they should see they have no power over the challenging behaviour. Without this power they have no responsibility for the challenging behaviour and its impacts and effects.

The individual with challenging behaviour and others around them are not responsible. Its not their fault. If they have no fault they are not to blame. If they are not to blame they should have no shame.

Once individuals with challenging behaviour and others around them learn that they are not to blame and they should have no shame they will begin to feel shame less and thus avoid the potential impact of shame on the feelings and attitudes of themselves and all these around them.

Hopefully as time goes by modern society will become more understanding of individuals with challenging behaviour and the people who love and care for them. For with that understanding there will be less ignorance and from that less shame, as more people understand challenging behaviour.

Rather than seen as 'wrong', 'strange', 'embarrassing' or 'sinful' challenging behaviour should be seen for what it is, challenging, without blame or responsibility. If an individual with challenging behaviour and other around them are not to blame they should receive no shame. As Jesus said "Let he who is without sin cast the first stone."

Long Term potential impacts on an individual with challenging behaviour and others feelings and attitudes.

Challenging behaviour will not just impact an individuals feelings and attitudes of all those around them over the short term. Where the individual or those around them may become angry or feel despair. There are potentials for impacts on the attitudes and feelings of the individual with challenging behaviour and others around them in the long term too.

Social Exclusion

The individual with challenging behaviour or their family and friends may become socially excluded leading to loneliness and depression.

Health

The individual with challenging behaviour or others around them may become unwell due to exhaustion and lack of rest in dealing with the challenging behaviour.

Cannot continue to care

The family or carer can make the decision that they cannot carry on caring for an individual with challenging behaviour and they would have to move permanently. Causing a potential impact to the individual and those around them with their feelings and attitudes over the long term.

Family ties broken, lives changed, and a great deal of questions with very few answers.

The Challenging Behaviour Foundation

I am sure that Vivien Cooper who founded the **Challenging Behaviour Foundation (CBF)** in 1997 on behalf of her child who displayed challenging behaviour, has faced the many potential impacts on her own feelings and attitudes as well as her own child and the people around them. Both short and long term. To the point of creating the only organisation for people with severe learning difficulties with challenging behaviour.

Vivien's aim should be our aim, to make a difference to the lives of the individual with challenging behaviour and those around them by being **aware** and **understanding** of the potential impacts to an individual and others feelings and attitudes by providing **support** and **imparting information**. Thus making a positive difference to their lives.

Section 2

Answer to Q12: Identify how to recognise changes in individuals that may indicate an episode of challenging behaviour.

Prevention is better than cure as the old saying goes, and if challenging behaviour can be prevented from happening then that in itself is cure. Yet the key to preventing challenging behaviour, if it is possible, is being able to recognize when and why an episode of challenging behaviour takes place.

To work out 'how' to recognise changes in individuals that may indicate an episode of challenging behaviour. You need to recognise changes in the individual with challenging behaviour. In order to identify how to recognise changes in individuals that may indicate an episode of challenging behaviour to prevent it or better understand it, it is advisable to:

Keep a diary and make notes about what happens before challenging behaviour is presented.

Are there any patterns to the challenging behaviour, does it occur at certain times or in similar circumstances. Once you have identified a pattern the triggers can become known and techniques can be put in place to prevent it.

Triggers and patterns

Once you have identified a pattern you can identify the triggers of the challenging behaviour and reduce the challenging behaviour. It is important to ask yourself eight basic questions:

1)   How does behaviour change before challenging behaviour is displayed.

Recognising changes in an individuals behaviour before challenging behaviour is presented can show what if anything has caused the challenging behaviour to occur. A change in behaviour before challenging behaviour is displayed can have a pattern and also be a trigger, as it would indicate a display of challenging behaviour is forthcoming. For example a dementia patient who you notice shakes her hands violently moments before having a screaming fit. Once you see those hands shake you know that the volcano is going to explode and you have a very short time to avoid a display of challenging behaviour, thus the behaviour change occurs so closely to a display of challenging behaviour that it becomes a trigger or in other individuals a certain change of behaviour psychologically triggers a display of challenging behaviour. In any event noticing the changes gives you much needed clues to adapt and begin dealing with the challenging behaviour.

2)   Are there any warning signs?

Does the individual with challenging behaviour have warning signs of a display of challenging behaviour. Do they begin to rock or say specific words? Do they begin to breath heavy? Is there a pattern to these warning signs. The warning signs themselves are communicating with you, they are warning you that challenging behaviour is imminent.

Warning signs themselves are triggers, identifying any warning signs will help you detect and prevent the onset of challenging behaviour.

3)   Are there certain situations that trigger displays of challenging behaviour.

Does the individual with challenging behaviour have a pattern. Are there certain situations that can be identified that make the challenging behaviour happen. Are there certain situations that 'trigger' the displays of challenging behaviour.

Does the challenging behaviour happen at specific places or with specific people. Does it happen only at work or school or at home.

Working out the pattern of the specific situations means you can then see what triggers the challenging behaviour and thus prevent it.

4)   Can the behaviour be linked to certain person/people.

Is there a pattern to the display of challenging behaviour. Can it be linked to a certain person or people. Do they trigger a display of challenging behaviour. Does a patient display challenging behaviour to a specific carer. Does the individual with challenging behaviour display the challenging behaviour only to the police. Identifying any patterns to challenging behaviour being displayed to certain persons or groups of people can help prevent the challenging behaviour being displayed.

5) **Is it a new behaviour that they are exhibiting**.

If it is a new behaviour when did it start, what has changed to cause the behaviour? Is it a sign in a deterioration of health? Identifying the change in the individual can be key to increasing their care.

6) **Is it a learned behaviour they are exhibiting**.

Did the individual with challenging behaviour learn to display the challenging behaviour. If you can identify that you can then identify why they displayed challenging behaviour and what is teaching the individual that behaviour. With that you can better care for the individual with challenging behaviour.

7) **Are there any particular events that trigger the behaviour.**

Such as a healthcare appointment or a trip to a noisy shopping centre for example.

Identifying particular events that trigger displays of challenging behaviour and recognising how the events change an individuals behaviour allows you to help control the displays of challenging behaviour.

An individual with challenging behaviour can act up on dentist trips leading you to look at pain or the fear of the dentist to trigger displays of challenging behaviour.

An individual with challenging behaviour could display challenging behaviour at a noisy shopping centre because of hypersensitivity to the noise which causes discomfort that leads to displays of challenging behaviour.

8)   **What happens after the behaviour**.

This question is perhaps the most important one. What happens after the behaviour stops. What caused the behaviour to stop. This 'cause' could be the answer you are seeking. Whatever made the individual with challenging behaviour to stop displaying challenging behaviour should be identified, as that knowledge can greatly help the individual with challenging behaviour control their challenging behaviour.

Also recognising changes in an individuals behaviour by noting what happens after a display of challenging behaviour informs you of a happy fact. That you can say with some certainty that the display of challenging behaviour has ended and the individual with challenging behaviour is better focused to receive care.

Answer to Q13: Explain the importance of identifying patterns of behaviour and triggers to challenging behaviour.

Identifying patterns of behaviour

The importance of identifying patterns of behaviour and triggers to challenging behaviour are some of the most important keys to opening the lock of cure for the individual with challenging behaviour.

Identifying patterns and triggers to challenging behaviour can help answer many important questions regarding the causes of the individuals challenging behaviour.

A patient has challenging behaviour but why? Identifying patterns can help answer that question.
If the individual with challenging behaviour displays challenging behaviour in a predictable pattern, their behaviour can be predicted and therefore controlled.

Forewarned is forearmed and if you can predict displays of challenging behaviour you can be ready for it. You will be prepared. You will not be surprised by it and will be ready to deal with it to the betterment of all, the individual with challenging behaviour, their carers and family.

Patterns of behaviour can help revel the causes of challenging behaviour not just in their predictability but also their type.

If a type of behaviour has a pattern it can inform you of the cause or reason for its existence. A man who becomes forgetful frequently and becomes agitated at his memory loss may be beginning to suffer symptoms of dementia.

A baby with toilet issues at the noisy shopping centre may have hypersensitivity. Such types of behaviour in a pattern can reveal possible autism for example.

Triggers to challenging behaviour

Triggers to displays of challenging behaviour are also important tools in predicting challenging behaviour, for example a dental appointment is due and a trip to the dentist triggers the individual with challenging behaviour, so you know that a display of challenging behaviour is forthcoming.

As well as controlling challenging behaviour, since you know the individual with challenging behaviour will display challenging behaviour and why. You can put in place techniques to control and reduce it until you can prevent it.

The importance of identifying patterns of behaviour and triggers to challenging behaviour are such that by doing so you benefit the individual with challenging behaviour, their carers, their families and their friends. Since with its correct application you can reduce stress both to the individual with challenging behaviour and others around them. You also reduce the chances of injury to the individual with challenging behaviour and others around them. Reduce barriers around the individual with challenging behaviour and improve their chances of social integration to the betterment of all.

It is important to try to act promptly to resolve challenging behaviour as many challenging behaviours can become more intense and harder to change if left unresolved. Without identifying patterns of behaviour or what triggers the individual with challenging behaviour, the prompt resolution of the challenging behaviour can become an impossibility.

With identification of patterns of behaviour and triggers to challenging behaviour the impossible becomes possible. Only with correct identification of patterns of behaviour and triggers to challenging behaviour will it become possible to promptly resolve challenging behaviour.

Once a pattern of challenging behaviour is identified it becomes possible to diagnose its cause. The 'reason' for the behaviour. Once that reason is established it is possible to look for other ways to meet the needs of the individual with challenging behaviour so that they do not resort to the displays of challenging behaviour.

Patterns and triggers to challenging behaviour allow you to diagnose the problem, from diagnosis
can come the cure. Identifying patterns of behaviour and triggers to challenging behaviour allows you to promptly resolve challenging behaviour.

Challenging behaviour can put an **individual at risk, cause injury to others, disrupt home life, prevent the individual from taking part in education, social and leisure activities** and **affect an individuals development and their ability to learn**.

Identifying patterns of behaviour and triggers to challenging behaviour allows the prompt resolution of challenging behaviour thus putting the individual at less risk, less disruption, less social exclusion, and increases their ability to learn, in short a better life! What's more important than that!

Children who have experienced traumatic life events

Special care must be made of children who have experienced traumatic life events, including loss and bereavement. According to Daniel, Cole, Sellmen, Sutton and Visser in their 2003 study they found that challenging behaviour from children who suffered traumatic life events was not uncommon.

Understanding and identifying triggers of challenging behaviour

Understanding and identifying triggers of challenging behaviour can reveal that ones own actions could trigger an incident of challenging behaviour.

For example:

A) **Rushing an individual with challenging behaviour to get ready to complete a task**.

You could be unknowingly putting too much pressure on an individual with challenging behaviour thus triggering a display of challenging behaviour.

B) **Trying to force an individual to eat foods they do not like**.

You may be making the individual with challenging behaviour have a display of challenging behaviour over limiting their life choices and their freedom.

C) **Shouting at a person when they do not do what you ask them to do**.

The individual with challenging behaviour may get frightened as they perceive aggressive behaviour or retaliate and get angry thus possibly displaying challenging behaviour.

D) **Denying an individual with challenging behaviour something they want as you haven't got the time**.

Again some individuals with challenging behaviour can get angry and display challenging behaviour at something denied without a good reason, again life options and freedoms will feel limited. An individual with challenging behaviour can feel frustrated since they will perceive the problem to be you not them, as it is you who does not have the time to help them. You will be perceived as a carer who doesn't care.

E)   **Forcing them into an environment they don't like**.

Nobody likes to be 'forced' to do anything and an individual with challenging behaviour can easily display challenging behaviour if they feel 'forced' to do something, as they may not understand why they have to be in an environment they don't like or become frustrated and angry at having their options and choices limited because they cannot say no.

F)   **Talking about an individual with challenging behaviour when they can hear you**.

Talking about somebody when you know they can hear you is rude and makes them upset why would it be different for individuals with challenging behaviour.

It wouldn't, individuals with challenging behaviour can become upset or angry that other people are knowing their business, forming negative attitudes about them, or feel demeaned as they are being talked about as an object with no care or respect for their presence, which should show they are a person with interests, feelings and attitudes. The individual with challenging behaviour will feel like an object in the room. Talked about but not talked too.

G)   **Ignoring them when they need attention**.

An individual with challenging behaviour can easily display challenging behaviour if you ignore them when they need attention.

Where is the care if you don't care, if you ignore the individual with challenging behaviour what is the point of anything you are trying to achieve through care plans, consultations, and goals when you ignore an individual with challenging behaviour when they need attention. Displays of challenging behaviour can easily occur because the individual with challenging behaviour can become angry and frustrated that they are not being listened to, and if they need attention, they are asking for help and you are not helping, you are ignoring, so you don't care.

H)   Trying to make them wear something they don't like.

An individual with challenging behaviour can display challenging behaviour when forced to do something they do not like or makes no sense to them such as being forced to wear certain clothes. They can become angry and frustrated at a lack of control of their own lives and a limitation of life choices. After all it's their clothes, they should be the ones to decide what they wear. Everybody else does so why not them.

Also the individual with challenging behaviour may not like the clothes for a reason, maybe it makes them itch, maybe it makes them remember tragic life events or other triggers.

I)   Exposing them to a person they find frightening or threatening.

An individual with challenging behaviour can display challenging behaviour like all of us if we become frightened or feel threatened.

A display of challenging behaviour would be a certainty in this situation and even provoke new challenging behaviour.

The individual with challenging behaviour could display fear at the situation, anger or aggression at the person they feel threatened by. The individual with challenging behaviour may runaway, scream, do literally anything.

These situations and that 'care' can go beyond ignoring (don't care) to outright harming the care of the individual with challenging behaviour, destroying trust and not being seen as just neutral but as an enemy. Actively placing the individual with challenging behaviour in jeopardy by forcing them into frightening and threatening situations and close to frightening and threatening people.

In the mind of the individual with challenging behaviour you the carer would have crossed Emerson's law, you yourself are placing somebody in jeopardy, and you will no longer be a trigger for displays of challenging behaviour from others but will become your own challenging behaviour through your actions of placing the individual with challenging behaviour in jeopardy.

The carer would become the one who needs care.

J)   **Constantly telling them not to do something**.

An individual with challenging behaviour can display challenging behaviour such as anger and frustration as they may feel their options are limited and their desires are being denied. They may also feel rebellious and stubborn if they feel entitled to what is being denied them. They also may not like being nagged like a world weary husband with a nagging wife.

The impact and effects of you

When looking for triggers to displays of challenging behaviour you must also look at yourself and your own actions with the individual with challenging behaviour.

\You are providing care and impacting the individuals life. It is up to you to provide good care or bad care. With positive actions you provide good care, with good care you have less chance of triggering displays of challenging behaviour.

The actions or triggers above are examples of bad care, rushing, forcing, shouting, little time, more forcing, rude, even more rude, more forcing, placing the patient in dangerous and frightening places with dangerous and frightening people. A carer whose only lexicon is 'no' and a nagger to boot!

Who on earth would want to be placed into such a persons care. It is not enough to say you care. Start to care. Actions speak louder than words.

Answer to Q14: Explain the importance of supporting individuals to recognise their own limitations and take avoidance actions.

Without support the house will fall. So it is with houses it is with individuals with challenging behaviour.

If one does not support an individual with challenging behaviour recognise their limitations and take avoidance actions, one does not help, quite the reverse one hinders.

To help, to support individuals recognise their own limitations and take avoidance actions, helps them, help themselves. Without such help an individual with challenging behaviour may be unable to take any responsibility on exercising any control over their own lives and would unlikely be able to live without constant support.

An individual with challenging behaviour who can be taught to recognise their own limitations should be supported, for a man should know his own limits. If an individual with challenging behaviour recognises that something's are too hard or even beyond them they will understand that help is needed and not display challenging behaviour.

"Only a fool fights a battle he cannot win" Genghis Khan

If individuals with challenging behaviour are supported to recognise their own limitations and manage their own feelings and behaviours, their quality of life will improve. If an individual with challenging behaviour can take avoidance actions they will be less reliant on others and be more likely to have some independence.

Just as families and carers need to learn to recognise their own limitations, as a man can only do so much, for the benefit of themselves and those around them, so must the individual with challenging behaviour.

The individual with challenging behaviour can be taught to recognise problems that lead to displays of challenging behaviour.

The individual with challenging behaviour can be taught the triggers that causes displays of challenging behaviour and avoid them. Less challenging behaviour, less problems.

Here is an example of the importance of supporting individuals to recognise their own limitation and take avoidance actions. To help them help themselves.

An individual with challenging behaviour becomes unsettled by noisy and busy environments and becomes stressed. This results in displays of challenging behaviour such as screaming or kicking out in the shopping centre.

The individual with challenging behaviour can be taught to recognise this and be supported to understand their limitations that there are some environments that are too noisy and busy for them. That there are some times and environments that over challenge them.

Once they recognise their own limitations they can take avoidance actions, the individual with challenging behaviour can help their stress and avoid situations that trigger the stress and its resultant displays of challenging behaviour.

So one of the avoidance actions that can be taken once the individual with challenging behaviour recognises their limitations of noise and busy places is to avoid places and situations that can be too noisy and busy for them.

Since the individual with challenging behaviour can recognise their limitations with noise and they can be supported by being provided headphones and soothing music to block out the noise and distress. Enabling the individual with challenging behaviour to have some independence.

Is it important to support individuals to recognise their own limitations or triggers to take avoidance action? The clear answer is yes.

Supporting individuals with challenging behaviour to recognise their limitations or triggers to take avoidance actions can:

1) **Give them more independence**.

2) **Enable them to continue to use the services they need**.

3) **Allow them to take part in activities**.

4) **Enable them to stay in an educational setting**.

5) **Minimize harm and injury to themselves and others**.

6) **Minimize disruption for others for example at school or collage**.

7) **Avoid punitive measures such as punishment or even dealing with the criminal justice   system**.

8) **Improve their own well being**.

9) **Reduce their need for constant care and supervision**.

10) **Improve their living arrangements by reducing conflict with others**.

11) **Enable them to take part in everyday routines and aspects of life such as shopping, eating out, social activities and use of public transport**.

Independence, continuity of quality care, social acceptance, opportunity to learn, lowering risk of injury and harm to themselves and those around them, giving themselves and those around them an easier life. **Now that's important!**

Answer to Q15: Describe strategies that could be used to support positive behaviour

With so many negative challenging behaviours it is important to **encourage positive behaviour** or in other words **support it**. This encouragement and support leads to a betterment of life for the individual with challenging behaviour and those around them, reducing stress and pressure, reducing risk of illness and injury, and reduce social isolation of the individual with challenging behaviour.

To support positive behaviour it is also important to have strategies in place to help you support positive behaviour.

Strategy Basics:

1)   **Your strategies need to be flexible and personalised to meet the needs of the people   involved**.

2)   **The support needs to prevent behaviour developing or getting worse**.

3)   **Your strategies for support should be in place before a crisis develops**.

4)   **There needs to be a clear plan, setting out the support needed for an individual**.

These strategies will help you deal with common problems caused by challenging behaviour. Often an individual with challenging behaviour will display challenging behaviour if they are not able to understand what is happening around them, or cannot communicate their wants and needs with others.

23

Challenging behaviour then is displayed commonly if the individual with challenging behaviour is confused or cannot communicate effectively thus leading to frustration. Strategies that reduce or eliminate confusion and lack of communication will help greatly to support the individual with challenging behaviour.

If there is **person centred and a positive behaviour support approach** rather than an **institutionalised centred approach** then the need for **'restrictive interventions'** such as **restraints, antipsychotic medication** or **seclusion/isolation,** is reduced.

Your strategies for supporting positive behaviour should emphasise the **respect of the individual** and **improving the quality of their lives**.

Positive Methods

Your strategy for supporting positive behaviour should include positive methods. Positive methods are used to teach the individual with challenging behaviour new positive behaviours to replace the challenging behaviours that they display.

For example if you have a child who has developed a learned response of kicking the table and screaming to get attention because the child wants the toilet. You can teach the child to ask for the toilet when they need it instead of using the learned response. This replacement of challenging behaviour with positive behaviour helps the individual with challenging behaviour and all those around them.

The starting point of your strategy is to understand 'why' the individual displays the challenging behaviour. Knowing 'what' the triggers are, then putting the support in place to prevent it happening or knowing what action to take to support the individual if the situation reoccurs.

Your strategies quite often will include changes to the individual with challenging behaviour 's environment. Positive behaviour support is quite often about **making changes to the environment**. As environmental factors are often triggers to displays of challenging behaviour.

Your strategies that could be used to support positive behaviour may require **teaching new skills**. For example communication skills if this is an issue for the individual with challenging behaviour.

This not only helps the individual with challenging behaviour replace challenging behaviour with positive behaviour but empowers the individual with challenging behaviour. The individual can see a positive future rather than a static present.

Your strategies to support positive behaviour may need to include **removing the need for attention seeking**, if this is the cause of displays of challenging behaviour.

Function of the behaviour

When seeking your strategies for supporting positive behaviour it is useful to consider the function of the behaviour displayed by the individual.

If it is challenging behaviour from an individual with some control over their behaviour 'why' are they doing it. What is the function of the behaviour.

1) **Is it to get attention**?

Why does the individual with challenging behaviour want attention? If that is the case are there triggers and causes of challenging behaviour from that need for attention. Is it something simple like a toilet break or trust issues where a patient only likes one nurse because they feel the other nurses treat them poorly.

2) **Is it to escape or avoid something or someone**?

Why does the individual with challenging behaviour want to escape somewhere or avoid some particular people or places. As before this challenging behaviour clues you in on possible triggers and causes of the challenging behaviour.

3) **Is it to get something tangible**?

What does the individual with challenging behaviour want. Maybe the cause for the display of challenging behaviour is simple maybe the individual with challenging behaviour wants a drink or some food. Strategies can be put in place to resolve the causes of displays of challenging behaviour and ultimately resolve the challenging behaviour itself once you give the individual with challenging behaviour what they desire or get them to understand that they cannot have what they desire for whatever reason.

4) **Is it to get a sensory need met**?

Does the individual with challenging behaviour like loud music, do they switch off the light constantly, do they prefer busy active social environments or very quiet environments.

Maybe the individual with challenging behaviour is autistic and has hypo-sensitivity and needs extra stimulus. Is the individual with challenging behaviour deaf, displaying challenging behaviour when they cannot hear words properly, or batteries from the hearing aid have become flat. Is the individual with challenging behaviour hypersensitive to sensory stimulus. Do they want peace and quiet, the light off and the music down.

Such challenging behaviour again gives clues to its cause and its triggers.

Here are some examples of positive behaviour supports for challenging behaviour for each of the **common four functions of behaviour**.

Example 1:

Dan becomes agitated at the residential home and starts to throw things at people.

Consulting with Dan and others around him you discover he does not like too many people around him and wishes to escape them or avoid them.

The function of his challenging behaviour is to escape or avoid the people.

You can help Dan by having some positive behaviour supports in place:

1) **Teach Dan some words and signs so Dan can show when he is becoming stressed**.

This will let you know the imminent triggers of a display of challenging behaviour and take steps to avoiding it.

2)   **Provide a flash card that Dan can show when he feels unhappy so he can be taken out of the lounge and into a quiet area.**

3)   **Learn to introduce Dan to groups of people slowly, to build up his tolerance.**

4)   **Use techniques to distract Dan when the lounge becomes busier, provide an activity like a board game or puzzle for example.**

Example 2:

Shannan lives in a small unit for six adults with a communal kitchen and living area. There has been problems with Shannan entering private bedrooms and stealing food and other belongings.

Consulting with Shannan we discover the **function of the behaviour.** Which is that Shannan **wants something tangible.** He wants food and other peoples things.

The positive behaviour supports that can be put in place as part of your strategy to support positive behaviour are:

1)   **Teach Shannan where food and other items he wants are kept using visual supports if needed.**

2)   **Give Shannan what he asks for if he requests food and drinks, etc.**

3)   **Teach Shannan appropriate ways to communicate what he wants.**

4)   **Give Shannan praise when he asks for things in an appropriate way**.

5)   **Make sure what he wants is easy to access**.

Example 3:

Grant hits other teenagers and adults at school.

Consulting with Grant and others around him you discover that he does this if he feels he is not noticed or he feels left out.

The function of his behaviour is attention seeking.

The positive behaviour supports that you can put in place can be:

1)   **Be aware of when Grant needs attention and if he tries to attract attention in an appropriate way, if that is the case you should meet Grant's needs as soon as possible**.

This supports his positive behaviour of asking for attention in an appropriate way and being rewarded for his positive behaviour by having his needs met quickly. Teaching Grant that it is far better to ask appropriately rather than become violent.

2)   **Teach Grant appropriate ways of attracting attention such as a sign, speaking to a person rather than hitting them, or to use a gentle tap on the arm to gain attention**.

3)   **Have a sign to show to Grant when he tries to hit someone, to show it is not appropriate**.

4)   **Give enough contact and interaction with Grant to allow him to get the attention he needs**.

Example 4:

Lucy kicks and hits out at home.

Through consulting Lucy and others around her you discover that Lucy is autistic which leads to a discovery that Lucy is Hypo-sensitive and that Lucy kicks out to provide herself with some stimulation.

The function of Lucy's behaviour is sensory need.

The positive behaviour supports that you can put in place can be:

1)   **You can provide other activities for Lucy to receive the stimulation she needs such as a ball or punchbag or a drum.**

2)   **You can provide routines where Lucy can take part in activities in a safe way.**

3)   **Involve an occupational therapist with a specialism in sensory needs, to carry out an assessment to identify Lucy's exact needs.**

Positive Behaviour Support

Here are some strategies to provide positive behaviour support:

1)   **Manage the way you communicate**.

Stay calm, control your body language, avoid too much eye contact.

2)   **Make changes to the environment**.

Is it too hot, noisy or bright for example.

3)   **Provide the individual with an activity they enjoy to distract them**.

4)   **Teach appropriate communication skills and body language**.

5)   **Put boundaries in place to teach the individual with challenging behaviour what's acceptable and where**.

6)   **Use rewards and incentives to encourage positive behaviour**.

7)   **Ignore or don't respond to the displays of challenging behaviour so the individual with challenging behaviour does not use their displays of challenging behaviour to gain attention**.

8)   **Distract the individual for example by using humour, a useful tool to avoid embarrassment**.

Descriptive Praise

Another strategy to support positive behaviour is descriptive praise. Telling the individual with challenging behaviour that you are happy, that they have done well and why they have done well.

Descriptive praise is a method of guiding an individual with challenging behaviour towards positive or desired behaviour. Rather than the usual phrases such as 'well done' or 'that's wonderful'. Descriptive praise states exactly what the individual with challenging behaviour has done that was good. The individual with challenging behaviour is informed of what behaviour is positive or desired.

Examples of descriptive praise:

1) **You've done what you were told straight away**.

2) **Well done! You sat on the train without shouting or getting up**.

3) **You've played with the others without hitting them**.

4) **You are speaking quietly now that you have stopped shouting**.

5) **You have eaten your food instead of playing with it**.

6) **You have stayed calm and not got angry**.

7) **You have tided up your things really well**.

8) **You have taken all your medicine without getting angry**.

Methods for recording information about an individuals behaviour

One of the strategies you could use for supporting positive behaviour is to use a method for recording information about an individuals behaviour. Such tools allow you to have a better understanding of the challenging behaviour. One such tool is the '**Antecedent, Behaviour and consequences recording chart**' known as **the ABC chart**.

Antecedent, Behaviour and Consequences recording chart

An **ABC chart** is an observational tool that allows us to record information about a particular behaviour. The aim of using an ABC chart is to better understand what the behaviour is communicating. The 'A' refers to the **antecedent** or **the event that occurred before the behaviour** was exhibited.

This can include what the person was doing, who was there, where they were, what sights / sounds / smells / temperatures / number of people that were in the environment.

'B' refers to an **objective and clear description of the behaviour that occurred** e.g. X threw item on the floor.

'C' refers to **what occurred after the behaviour** or the **consequence of the behaviour** e.g. children moved away from X, noise levels in the room decreased.

It is important to decide on one or two target behaviours to record initially. Place the ABC chart in an accessible place to make it easier to use after the target behaviour has been exhibited. Having recorded the behaviour on numerous occasions check for triggers or situations where the behaviour is most likely to occur: **When / what time is the behaviour most likely to occur? During what activities is the behaviour most likely to occur? Are there any times or activities during which the behaviour does not occur? Where is the behaviour most likely to occur? With whom is the behaviour most likely to occur?**

It is also important to look at **what consequences might be maintaining the behaviour: What does the behaviour achieve for the individual with challenging behaviour? Does the individual with challenging behaviour want to avoid or escape any activity by engaging in the behaviour? Is the individual with challenging behaviour rewarded in any way by engaging in the behaviour? What might the individual with challenging behaviour be attempting to communicate by engaging in this behaviour?**

Having identified the triggers for the behaviour and the consequences that may be maintaining the behaviour you are now ready to develop a plan.

1. What alternative or more appropriate skill can you teach the individual with challenging behaviour in order to eliminate their need to engage in this behaviour?

2. What changes can you make to the environment or the individual with challenging behaviour schedule in order to decrease their exposure to triggers?

3. How have you addressed the need that the individual with challenging behaviour was trying to communicate?

4. Is there any need for a reward / incentive scheme in the short-term?

5. Have you communicated your plan to everyone who will be caring for the individual with challenging behaviour?

ABC (Antecedent, Behaviour, Consequence) Chart

Form Date/Time:

Activity Antecedent Behaviour Consequence Date/Time:

When the behaviour occurred What activity was going on when the behaviour occurred:

What happened right before the behaviour that may have triggered the behaviour:

What the behaviour looked like:

What happened after the behaviour, or as a result of the behaviour:

Such tools as the ABC chart allows you to make a correct **functional assessment** of an individual with challenging behaviour.

With such strategies as positive behaviour support, changes in environment, detecting the function of behaviour, descriptive praise and the use of methods for recording information about an individuals behaviour such as the ABC chart. You will be well armed to support positive behaviour and in turn support the individual with challenging behaviour.

Answer to Q16: Explain the advantages of proactive strategies in supporting positive behaviour

Proactive strategies are those used to make sure the individual has what they need, and describe ways to teach the individual with challenging behaviour communication and other skills.

Proactive Strategies:

1) **Set boundaries**

2) **Have routine and structure in place**

3) **Offer rewards**

4) **Make adjustments to the environment for example dim lights, block out noises**

5) **Look for triggers**

6) **Teach the individual with challenging behaviour new skills for example have a sign for   finishing or ending an activity or conversation.**

7) **Be aware of how to talk to an individual with challenging behaviour, firmly, calmly etc.**

8) **Make interactions with the individual with challenging behaviour more positive.**

9) **Aim to teach the individual with challenging behaviour appropriate ways to seek   attention they need rather than using displays of challenging behaviour.**

10) **Provide the individual with challenging behaviour with more chances to practice and develop positive and appropriate behaviours. Practice makes perfect.**

11) **Give the individual with challenging behaviour structure and daily routines to cause less disruption to their lives and those around them.**

In fact these daily routines are probably one of the most important parts of your proactive strategies you put in place for the benefit of the individual with challenging behaviour. Proactive strategies are designed to minimise challenging behaviour and eliminate problems before they occur. **A successful behaviour plan should include more proactive strategies than reactive strategies.**

Note: **Proactive strategies are designed for before displays of challenging behaviour occurs. Reactive are strategies designed for after displays of challenging behaviour occurs.**

Answer to Q17: **Explain the impact of reactive strategies in supporting positive behaviour**

Reactive strategies are as the name implies reactive. You are reacting to the individual with challenging behaviour. Therefore you are acting after the event and reactive strategies are strategies you have designed to cope with displays of challenging behaviour and its impacts and effects once it occurs and reduce the displays of challenging behaviour in the future.

The main focus of reactive strategies is to keep the individual with challenging behaviour and those around them safe.

Here are some examples of reactive strategies.

1)   **Provide reminders after the display of challenging behaviour or event**.

2)   **Give the individual with challenging behaviour what they need or want**.

3)   **Distract the individual with challenging behaviour from over challenging situations   when necessary**.

4)   **Remove yourself from the situation for example leave the room to allow the individual   with challenging behaviour to calm down**.

5)   **Don't respond to the displays of challenging behaviour. If it is a case of attention-   seeking**.

Reactive strategies are planned ways of responding to specific events and aim to deal with the behaviour after it happens.

They aim to provide responses that make challenging behaviour not desirable for the individual.

Early reactive strategies

Early reactive strategies are important as early intervention is important, as this can prevent challenging behaviour escalating. For example if an individual with challenging behaviour demands attention and is ignored the challenging behaviour is likely to escalate, but by providing attention early on the escalation can be prevented from becoming more disruptive.

Reactive strategies cannot be used solely to help deal with challenging behaviour and displays of challenging behaviour, you also need proactive strategies to accompany your tool set.

For example in the case of the individual with challenging behaviour with attention difficulties both proactive and reactive strategies are needed to provide them with the attention they need while also preparing the individual with challenging behaviour for times that they will be expected to cope without attention.

Consistent strategies

In addition to developing proactive and reactive strategies for the individual with challenging behaviour and teaching the individual with challenging behaviour through those strategies. It is important to get the team around the individual with challenging behaviour and the individuals family and friends on board to your strategies. So everyone has a consistent approach to the task. You can also watch the reactions of all those around the individual with challenging behaviour personally.

It is very helpful to ensure that everyone has a shared understanding of the function of the behaviour of the individual. Why the individual acts the way they do.

Let us look at a more detailed example showing proactive and reactive strategies to deal with an individual with challenging behaviour.

Jay constantly seeks attention from the teacher and if he doesn't get the attention he wants, his behaviour becomes challenging, affecting the learning of himself and others. You have to think about ways to provide the attention whilst also allowing the teacher to attend to the needs of the other pupils in the class.

The function of Jay's behaviour is attention seeking.

Proactive strategies for attention seeking.

1)   Appoint Jay as the book monitor, to hand out books and worksheets before tasks.

This is to distract Jay and give him something to do. Keeping him busy helps reduce Jay's desire for attention.

2)   Give Jay more attention before the whole class activity begins.

This gives Jay what he wants, attention, without affecting the whole class.

3)   Allow Jay to work with a partner for the last ten minutes if the lesson providing he has worked alone previously on a school task.

This eliminates the need for attention from the teacher as Jay will be receiving attention from another pupil in the class.

Also like appointing Jay as a book monitor this strategy also distracts Jay by giving him something to do. It's giving something for Jay to concentrate on rather than giving his attention needlessly to the teacher. He can focus on the job at hand. Finally this proactive strategy alleviates the boredom of Jay which is a big problem of individuals with attention deficit disorder. Change is as good as a rest.

a

4) **Before leaving Jay's immediate area to attend to other pupils the teacher should inform Jay that the teacher is going to be busy.**

This proactive strategy sets a boundary to the individual with challenging behaviour, preparing them for the period of time they will have to spend without any attention.

Reactive strategies for Jay include:

1) **Descriptive praise**

Give Jay plenty of descriptive praise, 'Well done Jay by being quiet with the others', 'Great Job Jay you did it all by yourself'.

2) **Rewarding desired behaviour**

Reward Jay with attention before and after the lesson. This makes Jay feel special and feeds his desire for attention.

3) **Planned ignoring**

React to Jay's challenging behaviour by ignoring it in set busy times, after you have informed him you will be busy remember to keep Jay informed about when busy times are and there duration. This will teach him not to demand attention during set times. Also you can not respond to Jay at other times until he has raised his hand.

4) **Redirection**

If signs of displays of challenging behaviour are imminent you can have a strategy in place to distract the individual with challenging behaviour. When Jay's challenging behaviour appears imminent or begins to display, you can give him something to distract him, for example hand out books, collect equipment etc.

Reactive strategies are 'actions, responses and planned interventions in response to the presentation of identifiable behaviour that challenges'. Reactive strategies have the aim of bringing about 'immediate behavioural change in an individual' or 'establishing control over a situation so that risk associated with the presentation of the behaviour is minimised or eradicated'. Reactive strategies may take a number of forms and can include environmental, psychosocial and restrictive interventions such as physical holds, mechanical and manual restraint, seclusion and 'time out' or the use of emergency medication. It is suggested "that up to half of people with a learning disability who display behaviour that challenges may be subject to reactive strategies." ('Supporting staff working with challenging behaviour' Paley and Brooke 2006).

Reactive strategies do not aim to achieve long-term behaviour change, however those strategies that are aversive or punitive have the potential to change an individual's behaviour through negative association with displaying particular behaviours. Much research in the 1970s and 1980s focused on alternatives to punishment and aversive strategies.

More recently interventions that focus on upholding an individual's human rights have come to the fore. Such approaches treat people with dignity and respect, have an ethical basis and are delivered alongside proactive strategies in order to reduce the likelihood of behaviour that challenges.

Reactive strategies are more likely to be effective in the context of good person-centred planning that recognises the situations, environment, social settings or interpersonal environments that are associated with a higher likelihood of behaviour that challenges and seeks to affect change in those settings.

Traditional behaviour support planning typically draws on a menu of reactive strategies including: environmental change; stimulus control, cessation or introduction; preferred activities; preferred interactions/people; distraction, diffusion and de-escalation.

Guidance issued on the subject of behavioural support, reactive strategies and restrictive practices has taken on a generic health and social care focus where previously specific guidance for people with a learning disability and behaviour that challenges was published. However, the focus has continued to be on the principles of least restrictive alternatives, proportionality to the risks posed by the behaviour and gradient approaches to any reactive or restrictive interventions, considering restrictive interventions only as a last resort.

Answer to Q18: Describe strategies to support individuals to manage their behaviour.

When individuals with challenging behaviour are happy they usually do not display negative challenging behaviour. Strategies that support individuals to manage their behaviour helps to make them happy.

When an individual with challenging behaviour displays challenging behaviour this often means something is not working for them and their needs are not being met. If we aim to make the individual with challenging behaviour happy and satisfied that their needs are being met then we will have less displays of challenging behaviour.

Strategies that support individuals manage their behaviour should include:

1)   Strategies that make the individual with challenging behaviour feel valued and makes them feel they are being treated with respect.

2)   Strategies that involve listening to the individual with challenging behaviour.

3)   If the individual with challenging behaviour has communication problems then strategies must be put in place to teach appropriate and alternative communication methods. So they do not resort to displays of challenging behaviour to get their needs met or to get attention.

4)   Strategies to teach the individual with challenging behaviour to recognise their own distress and the things that cause the distress and resultant stress.

This is useful to help you implement strategies to allow the individual with challenging behaviour to be given ways of dealing with stress and their distress as displays of challenging behaviour starts to happen but before the display develops into something more serious.

5)   Teach strategies of 'stress and distress recognition' to the individual with challenging behaviour's family and carers. So they can become aware of triggers and your proactive and reactive strategies, to avoid and cope with the impacts and effects of the displays of challenging behaviour.

Possible strategies to support individuals to manage their behaviour are:

1)   Develop ways in which the individual can deal with problems they face. For example, wearing headphones to listen to music if the individual with challenging behaviour does not like certain environments or noise. Have the individual with challenging behaviour practice breathing exercises to calm themselves down or have the individual with challenging behaviour learn techniques such as sitting on their hands if they feel they are going to hit out at others or throw things.

2)   Provide alternative communication methods for those whose displays of challenging behaviour are caused by a lack of communication skills, such as cards with faces or symbols to show what they are feeling or what they want.

3)   Help the individual to avoid challenging behaviour by creating the right environment for them. Strategies should be put in place to allow the individual with challenging behaviour avoid their triggers such as avoiding noise, bright lights, crowds, certain smells, etc.

4)   Provide activities and materials that can help to calm them or distract them.

5)   Make sure that expectations from the individual with challenging behaviour, their staff, their carers and their family are realistic, the individual with challenging behaviour should not be over challenged and be set up for a failure. Goals set for the individual with challenging behaviour need to be realistic and achievable.

In developing strategies to support individuals with challenging behaviour to manage their behaviour it is important that the families of the individual with challenging behaviour have:

1)   **The right knowledge**

2)   **That they share knowledge and expertise.**

3)   **That everyone involved works to provide consistent support, to deal with the behaviour   in the same way.**

4)   **The need to have an appropriate level of support and the need to provide a suitable   level of stimulation for the individual with challenging behaviour.**

The strategies to support individuals to manage their behaviour should be appropriate and suitable. The individual with challenging behaviour should not be bored but also should not be overwhelmed or over challenged. In developing strategies to support individuals to manage their behaviour it is important to teach new communication skills and coping strategies, along with descriptive praise, encouragement and reward for desired behaviour.

What your strategies and plans should do:

Your strategies to support individuals manage their behaviour should follow a plan. This plan should help support individuals by:

1)   **Allow you and others to have an understanding of what the individual is trying to achieve or communicate through their challenging behaviour.**

Your strategy or plan should allow you to understand what the individual with challenging behaviour wants or is telling you through their challenging behaviour. What is the function of their behaviour.

2)   **Your strategies and plans should be to make adaptations to the individual with challenging behaviours environment so you and others can better cater to the needs of the individual with challenging behaviour.**

3)   **Your strategies and plans to support individuals manage their behaviour should identify approaches that try to teach and encourage the individual to use new, more appropriate behaviours, and to cope with difficulties and tensions when his or her needs are not being immediately met. Like a form of insurance your care plan needs reactive and proactive strategies in case disaster strikes.**

4)   **Your care plan should have strategies for rewarding the individual with challenging behaviour when they display appropriate behaviour.**

The individual with challenging behaviour should understand when they have behaved correctly and be rewarded for it, to develop a learned response that appropriate behaviour is correct. After all you need the carrot to go with the stick.

5)   **Your care plan should have strategies that include planned responses that can be used when the individual displays challenging behaviour.**

Your reactive strategies to deal with challenging behaviour after it occurs will forearm you to be prepared and keep the challenging behaviour and its impacts and effects to a minimum.

Formulating your strategies to support individuals to manage their own behaviour

Some useful points when formulating your strategies to support individuals to manage their own behaviour within your care plan:

1)   **Every individual is unique**. What works with on one individual with challenging behaviour may not work with another with similar behaviour. A care plan and strategies used for a previous individual with challenging behaviour with the same behaviour or function of behaviour may not work as well as it did before.

2)   **Make sure that your care plan and strategies are consistent** and consistently established by all others involved in the care of the individual.

3)   **Organise the environment of the individual** with challenging behaviour and adapt it if necessary to reduce the chances of challenging behaviour being displayed and avoid things that trigger it.

4)   **Your care plan should have strategies to support the individual** with challenging behaviour to manage their behaviour by providing structure and predicability.

Ever changing routines and events can over challenge the individual with challenging behaviour and trigger anxiety and displays of challenging behaviour.

5) **Your care plan should include strategies to support the individual** with challenging behaviour manage their behaviour by **establishing and repeating rules clearly and using clear guidelines**.

The individual with challenging behaviour has to hear and understand why they are executing your strategies otherwise they can become confused and you will only be adding to the stress.

6) **Use visual prompts such as flash cards for those struggling with communication**.

This can be a quick and convenient way of communicating and help the individual with challenging behaviour manage their behaviour.

7) **Focus on the positive**.

The individual with challenging behaviour are often on the receiving end of a lot of negative comments from people around them in society.

The individual with challenging behaviour often feel depressed and feel bad about themselves with natural feelings of shame, guilt or depression. This is likely to make the challenging behaviour worse. It can help an individual with challenging behaviour manage their behaviour by staying positive.

8)   **The label of the condition is not the individual**.

The challenging behaviour is not the individual, it is the individual that has the behaviour. The behaviour is a part of the individual that will be resolved by the individual managing their behaviour, it is not the whole.

9)   **Reminding**

Your strategies should include reminders of rules when the individual with challenging behaviour starts to display challenging behaviour I.e. "Jay, the rule is that we wait our turn in the canteen line".

Check that the individual with challenging behaviour hears and understanding you. The rule on reminding is to help the individual with challenging behaviour to learn your strategies and help the individual with challenging behaviour to learn your strategies and help the individual with challenging behaviour manage their behaviour.

10)   **Descriptive praise after a display of challenging behaviour**.

Your strategies to support individuals with challenging behaviour manage their behaviour should include strategies for descriptive praise at the earliest opportunity to diffuse displays of challenging behaviour. So it is best to catch them displaying appropriate behaviour and praising them for it especially with appropriate behaviour following displays of challenging behaviour.

11)   Describe behaviours that you do want to see.

By describing the behaviours you want to see displayed by the individual explains to the individual the types of behaviour that are wanted. Remember to keep things positive   do not focus on negative challenging behaviour.

I.e.:   "Jay I don't want you to eat all the sachets of porridge today", instead of "Jay! Stop stealing other peoples food!".

12)   Descriptive praise to reinforce positive behaviour.

By descriptively praising the individual with challenging behaviour when they keep to the rules you have set. I.e. "Jay, I like the way you have tidied your plate away".

13)   Look for opportunities to praise positive behaviour.

Increase your focus on the positive by trying to catch the individual with challenging behaviour behaving in a positive way. I.e.: "Jay, it was really good that you stayed calm and sorted out the discussion. Thank you for choosing that appropriate behaviour."

It is important that the individual with challenging behaviour feels they have a choice, the freedom and control, the belief that they can manage their own behaviour. Focusing on immediate descriptive praise of positive behaviour after displays of challenging behaviour helps achieve this.

14) **Precise descriptive praise**

You should use precise descriptive praise to describe exactly what the individual with challenging behaviour has done that warrants the praise. I.e.: "Well done Jay for staying in your seat". Rather than non descriptive which could be construed as patronisation. I.e. "Good Boy!".

Possible strategies to support individuals to manage their behaviour.

Example:

Glenn doesn't like his cousins due to problems in their childhood and now as an adult he becomes stressed when they visit or at present at family events. He starts to swear and throw things at them so some family members have said they would prefer Glenn not to attend any family events.

Possible ways to support individuals to manage their behaviours.

The function of Glenn's behaviour is avoidance. He has told you and as can clearly be seen that he wants to avoid his cousins. Maybe there was a traumatic life event in Glenn's past or maybe Glenn was under constant bullying.

Something you can do to support Glenn in managing his behaviour.

1)   Avoid his cousins

Advise that Glynn should avoid his cousins since they appear to be triggering his challenging behaviour.

2)   Keep Glenn's family and carers informed.

Inform Glenn's family and carers because of the problems and stress that Glynn receives from being triggered by being around his cousins that Glynn can still be involved in family activities and gathering as long as his cousins are not in attendance.

The family must understand that only the cousins are the issue and Glynn should not be punished by being made the family outcast and therefore suffer from being socially isolated.

3)   Strategies to unplanned meeting of Glenn's cousins.

Should Glynn meet his cousins in unplanned circumstances strategies can be put in place for Glynn to go to a safe area or exercises to make him relax.

4)   Inform Glenn's cousins of your strategies

Glenn's cousins should be made aware that they are triggers to displays of Glenn's challenging behaviour, your strategies to help deal with the challenging behaviour and how serious the situation Glenn is in. Without the cousins help and understanding, dealing with Glenn will be much harder.

5) **Involve the rest of the family in your strategies**

The whole family should be informed and get together to support Glenn with understanding and consistency.

6) **Strategies to deal with displays of challenging behaviour.**

Strategies should be put in place to remind Glenn when he displays challenging behaviour.

7) **Group therapy.**

You can advise Glenn, his cousins and immediate family to undertake group therapy to discuss issues in a safe setting so that Glenn feels free to speak about his long standing issues without being over challenged or overly stressed.

When formulating strategies to support individuals to manage their behaviour bear in mind there is a correlation between challenging behaviour and the severity of a learning disabilities. There is an increased prevalence of challenging behaviour in people with severe learning disabilities.

Children with traumatic life events and those with severe learning difficulties

So as an aide-memoire children with traumatic life events and those with severe learning difficulties are more likely than others to have a display of challenging behaviour and as such this should alert you to take note of such individuals with these conditions.

Abusive strategies

Although there are many positive and appropriate strategies to support individuals with challenging behaviour manage their challenging behaviour, there are several strategies you should not adopt or condone. As rather than strategies to support the individual with challenging behaviour these strategies are in fact abuse that will damage the individual with challenging behaviour and could cause you yourself to be arrested.

1)   **Do not assault the individual with challenging behaviour.**

2)   **Do not restrain the individual with challenging behaviour harshly.**

3)   **Do not give the individual with challenging behaviour cold punishment showers.**

4)   **Do not leave the individual with challenging behaviour outside especially in near zero temperatures.**

5)   **Do not pour mouthwash into the eyes of the individual with challenging behaviour.**

6)   **Do not pull the individual with challenging behaviours hair.**

7)   **Do not force medication into the patients mouth.**

8)   **Do not poke the individual with challenging behaviour in the eyes.**

9)   **If an individual with challenging behaviour attempts to escape do not mock him.**

Although this seems like obvious advice incredibly it is true. Such 'care' as this is seen under the law as abuse and torture. This can lead to imprisonment of the carer as well as contravening the individual with challenging behaviours human rights under the **human rights act 1998**.

Article 5 of the Human Rights Act 1998 requires no one should be deprived of their liberty except in certain predefined circumstances. There must also be an appropriate legally based procedure in place to protect the individual with challenging behaviours rights.

The Care Quality Commission

All of the above was committed by paid professional carers at the Winterbourne View private hospital in south Gloucestershire in 2010/2011 as investigated by the BBC's Panorama program. The result was the carers in criminal trouble and the hospital was shut down.

It was this action that caused the Association of supported living to issue a press statement asking for community based supported living services to replace institutional based services for people with learning disabilities. They also wrote to every member of parliament urging a change in the law.

The result was the Care Quality Commission (CQC) finally did a nationwide check on all facilities owned by the same company that owned Winterbourne View hospital, **Castlebeck Care**. The check resulted in three further facilities being shut down.

CQC reported a systematic failure to protect people or to investigate allegations of abuse.

Castlebeck Care did not care, they did not care about the safety and welfare of the individuals with challenging behaviour in their care and they did not care that these same individuals may be receiving abuse. The CQC came under criticism for ignoring previous warnings of Winterbourne View hospital.

It is the Winterbourne View case and cases like it have led to recent law changes. The focus of care has been moved for individual with challenging behaviour from institutionally based care to community based supported living services. To the benefit of the individual with challenging behaviour.

Negative strategies

Therefore strategies that support individuals to manage their own behaviour should not only include positive strategies, descriptive praise, proactive strategies, reactive strategies, better environment, more time and attention etc. But avoid any care that can be considered negative, care that can lead to and is open to abuse. You the carer may unknowingly be abusing your patient by following some strategies too vigorously or with little regard to the individual with challenging behaviour.

For example:

1)	Ignoring can lead to an individual with challenging behaviour left outside in the garden safe space in sub-zero temperatures.

2)	Set boundaries can become the individual with challenging behaviour does not move from the chair.

Your routine and structure strategies for the individual with challenging behaviour may provide little or nothing for the individual with challenging behaviour. Quite the reverse your strategies could become an abusive prison sentence for the most vulnerable in society.

The Nazi backed T4 program which ended with the involuntary euthanasia of those deemed 'unfit for society' began with doctors thinking they knew best and the individual with challenging behaviour knows nothing.

Be careful with your strategies to support individuals with challenging behaviour. You are responsible for them not the individual with challenging behaviour. You make the strategies not the individual with challenging behaviour. The individual with challenging behaviour is following your advice and instructions. If you ever see a court over your strategies and care of the individual with challenging behaviour, You will be the one in the dock not the individual with challenging behaviour. Because under the eyes of the law you are responsible for your own strategies not the individual with challenging behaviour. The road to hell is paved with good intentions.

Answer to Q19: Explain how Behaviour Plans and Support Plans are used to support positive behaviour.

A behaviour and support plan is a step by step plan based on the individual with challenging behaviour and their characteristics and needs. The behaviour and support plan provides information about the individuals behaviour for the staff and professional carers who work with them.

A behaviour and support plan helps carers understand possible triggers and issues and puts strategies in place to deal with challenging behaviour and displays of challenging behaviour.

A behaviour and support plan is the skeleton onto which the muscles of your positive behaviour support, proactive and reactive strategies, and all the ideas you have to help the individual with challenging behaviour are attached to make a manageable whole.

The behaviour and support plan is the scripture of the individual with challenging behaviour's care and cannon for other staff members as it informs them of what to do in your absence or a golden reference should you be busy. It also remind you of what should be done and when.

All of your support strategies are fed into the behaviour and support plan so they may be executed properly. The behaviour and support plan is the centralisation of all your support strategies. It is the Gosplan (Soviet State Planning Committee) of your care, you can have strategies but you must have a behaviour and support plan. As the Russians would say the plan is the plan.

This centralisation of strategies helps swift and timely strategy execution consistently. This helps support positive behaviour from the individual with challenging behaviour. The clue is in the name behaviour support plans are there to support positive behaviour.

Behaviour Support Plan

A behaviour support plan must include the following:

1) **The main issues of the individuals behaviour**.

What is wrong with the patient. What are the challenging behaviours. This information informs you and the staff as to the main problems or issues regarding the individual with challenging behaviour.
This is your first step and base of your behaviour and support plan. Without knowing the main issues you cannot resolve them.

2) **Any conditions that are likely to trigger behaviour that challenges, such as a particular environment or person**.

Once you know the issues, your behaviour and support plan should have notes as to what triggers challenging behaviour from an individual so you can avoid them and deal with them. With proactive and reactive strategies and any relevant support strategies to deal with triggers.

3) **Your Behaviour and Support plan should include notes of warning signs that the individual is experiencing problems that are likely to lead to challenging behaviour**.

Your behaviour and support plan has these notes so you can avoid predictable situations likely to over-challenge the individual with displays of challenging behaviour. Does the individual with challenging behaviour not like noise, or crowds, bright lights. Then dense shopping areas or crowds should be avoided because this environment will over challenge the individual with challenging behaviour and cause a display of challenging behaviour to be triggered.

Also if you can see warning signs of an imminent display of challenging behaviour you can have strategies in place to deal with it.

4)   Your Behaviour Support plan should include positive supports for the individual.

Man cannot live on bread alone and no man is an island. Your behaviour and support plan must include positive behaviour support. That's the point. A behaviour support plan is there to support positive behaviour. No positive supports in your plan then you are unlikely to receive positive behaviour from the individual with challenging behaviour.

To paraphrase Charlton Heston in the film Soylant Green (1973) "individuals with challenging behaviour are people!"

Individuals with challenging behaviour are us only they have challenging behaviour. Like individual with challenging behaviour we appreciate the positive, the well done's, the good shows and a plan for the future. To be positive. We are told that if at first you don't succeed try, try and try again. We are not told "Just give up!".

So it is with the individual with challenging behaviour. There is little enough positive about the individuals situation when they meet you. Be positive include positive supports in your behaviour and support plan, descriptive praise, rewards, attention, proactive strategies that uplift the individual with challenging behaviour, boost their confidence, increase their opportunities and life choices. Include positive supports to increase the individual with challenging behaviour freedom.

Positive support strategies are fundamental in helping individuals with challenging behaviour manage their behaviour.

It is easier to help an individual with challenging behaviour with positive strategies than negative strategies. We are here to give ability to the individual with challenging behaviour to help make the disabled able once again. Positive support strategies within the behaviour support plan is a funder mental part of this ethos and excellent tools for success.

5)   A plan for diffusing the situation or behaviour.

Proactive strategies should be put in place within your behaviour and support plan to diffuse situations and avoid displays of challenging behaviour before the displays start or are triggered.

6)   Consistency

Your Behaviour and Support plan should include strategies that enable the staff, carers, family and the individual with challenging behaviour's peers to help the individual with challenging behaviour manage their behaviour and increase the understanding of the individual with challenging behaviour and others around them as to the nature of the challenging behaviour and what can be positively done to support the individual with challenging behaviour consistently.

7)   Support and encouragement

Your behaviour and support plan should include strategies as to what should do in common situations involving the individual with challenging behaviour to offer support and encouragement. This will help the individual with challenging behaviour by supporting their positive behaviour.

Behaviour and Support plan the need to know

Your behaviour and support plan needs to be read by the staff before they work with an individual with challenging behaviour so that all staff who encounters the individual with challenging behaviour are aware of how to create a positive and safe environment for the individual with challenging behaviour.

Your behaviour and support plan needs to have families and carers be aware of the plan. To have an effective behaviour care plan you need the support of families carers and peers. These people cannot support something in which they are unaware of.

Behaviour support plan collaboration and agreement

If possible the behaviour care plan should be drawn up in collaboration with staff and carers and families. All of the interested parties should have their say with the individual with challenging behaviour having the loudest voice. This collaborative method makes it easier for everybody to focus on choosing the most urgent behaviour issues to be tackled first.

Keep it simple!

If too many challenging behaviours are attempted to be dealt with at once the individual with challenging behaviour can become over challenged. and the care plan can become difficult to manage.

When choosing the behaviour that is in the most urgent need of resolution it is important to remember the well being of the individual with challenging behaviour and others is paramount before focusing on other issues or behaviours.

The individual with challenging behaviour and others around them must be safe or as Emerson (1995) so very long ago stated **"The physical safety of a person or others should not be placed in jeopardy"**.

After the well-being of the individual with challenging behaviour and those around them has been assured then you can focus on the easiest and simplest behavioural issues to resolve. Which behaviour has the most chance to be successfully dealt within the shortest possible time.

The quicker you get the individual with challenging behaviour to manage their own behaviour the better results you will have with your behaviour support plan.

Examples of behaviour support plans:

William attends a day centre to give his elderly parents some respite from his challenging behaviour. When William becomes stressed he becomes aggressive and your other staff have difficulty controlling him.

So it is time for a behaviour support plan to instruct your staff and better support Williams needs. To support Williams positive behaviour.

Here is the support plan for William.

Williams difficulties

1)   Noisy environments

William has told you that he does not like noises.

2)   Too many people in the room

William has told you he does not like too many people and the staff have noticed that too many people trigger his displays of challenging behaviour.

3)   Having a conversation in a group

You have noticed that William has trouble communicating and becomes stressed when he talks with more than one person at a time.

4)   The dining room when there are people around

Your staff informs you and you see for yourself that William displays challenging behaviour in the dining area when there are too many people.

Behaviour William might display

Early warning signs of William

1)   William begins to ignore people who try to talk to him.

You can see William is becoming over challenged. and stressed at too much going on, and when he begins to ignore people this usually brings a display of challenging behaviour.

2)   **William covers his ears**.

This is another early warning sign you and the staff note as a warning sign that William is becoming over challenged. and about to display challenging behaviour. William is letting you know it's noisy.

3)   **William holding his head**.

This is a common behaviour William does when he feels stressed and the environment is becoming over challenging.

4)   **William starts to rock and continue rocking**.

Another early warning sign of increased stress and being over challenged. leading to a common display of challenging behaviour.

What does William do if the early warning signs are ignored?

There are displays of challenging behaviour if Williams early warning signs are ignored:

1)   William screams and shouts.

2)   William begins to become violent and aggressive by hitting out others.

3)   William attacks staff.

4)   William throws things.

5)   William runs away.

This is all challenging behaviour which crosses **Emerson**'s line, **they either put the safety of the individual with challenging behaviour or others around him in jeopardy** or **behaviour likely to have him denied access to ordinary community facilities** because it is culturally abnormal/anti-social due to the behaviours **intensity, frequency or duration**. Thus it is these displays of challenging behaviour that have to be resolved or avoided hence the existence and execution of this behaviour and support plan so that it can help William support his positive behaviour and resolve and avoid his negative behaviour.

Support the positive and do not support the negative will help William mange his own behaviour.

How to avoid displays of Williams challenging behaviour:

Proactive strategies

1)   Limit the number of people around him

Too many people are a big problem for William. Amend his environment, have him go to dining areas and common rooms at quiet times. Inform the staff that it is best for one staff member to talk to William at one time, inform them of the issues of too many people and too much information over challenges William ad causes him stress which leads to challenging behaviour. Less people equals less problems.

2) **Allow William to eat lunch early**

Give William some control of his life and environment, empower William and give support to the positive behaviour of William by allowing him to eat his lunch in peace and away from a challenging environment. Avoid that noise and avoid all those people.

3) **Take William to a quiet, safe area if a lot of visitors are expected**.

Again avoid too many people and too much noise if too many people are expected with this proactive strategy.

4) **Give William a communication card to show when William becomes stressed**.

This proactive strategy again empowers Williams to show when he feels stressed and over challenged. This strategy within the behaviour and support plan supports his positive behaviour which in turn supports the individual to manage their own behaviour and supports William to recognize his own limitations and help him take avoidance actions.

This sort of strategy helps him understand himself better and communicate better.

To help him be aware of the stress and what it means it helps him have more control, as he is in control of the communication. It helps him because he can show his card and you will understand why he wants attention.

Strategies that help the individual with challenging behaviour

This 'help' is the ballast of your strategies. If you develop a strategy that does not help but hinders or creates problems outweighing the displays of challenging behaviour then it is a bad strategy for the individual with challenging behaviour and should be discarded.

If your strategy 'helps' in a number of ways by empowering the individual with challenging behaviour, by allow him to communicate better, avoids challenging environments without limiting the individual with challenging behaviour life choices then the strategy is of sufficient weight to be a good strategy.

Like fruit you should weigh and check your strategies soundness. A rotten apple you discard but a sweet one goes into the pie.

This is a fundamental question for your strategy, you must ask yourself with any of your strategies does it help?

Reactive strategies

It is one thing to have proactive strategies in place within you behaviour and support plan for staff to follow. But as proactive as you can be, as careful as you are, displays of challenging behaviour will occur. So while you have to be proactive and have proactive strategies in place you must also be ready in your behaviour and support plan to react to help support Williams positive behaviour.

Here are some reactive strategies to help William, by supporting his positive behaviour and help him manage his own behaviour.

1)   **Talk to William and distract him if the room becomes busy**.

This is a reactive strategy to help avoid displays of challenging behaviour by William, or limit the impact of his challenging behaviour.

2)   **Remind William about using his time out card**.

Support William in managing his own behaviour by reminding him that he can communicate his needs and issues.

3)   **Hold Williams hand if the dining room becomes busy**.

Holding the individual with challenging behaviour hand is one of mother natures most basic, obvious and powerful ways to communicate care to support the individual with challenging behaviour.
It is instinctual, mothers hold their children's hand, grandparents hold their grand children's hands, teachers and lollipop people hold children's hands crossing the road. It is an instinctual method of one human being caring for another and supporting them. This reactive strategy is very useful if used appropriately within your behaviour and support plan.

4)   **Give William a puzzle book or a jigsaw to take his mind off other people**.

This reactive strategy is used to distract the individual with challenging behaviour to avoid the immediate onset of challenging behaviour.

Prevention of future incidents

Consider Williams triggers to displays of challenging behaviour, how can they be prevented? What did William respond to? What calmed him down?

If displays of challenging behaviour escalates

1) **Staff and carers should speak to William calmly and quietly during and after displays of challenging behaviour**.

William needs to become calm, and understand why he is to be calm. The impact of his challenging behaviour needs to be limited to limit the effect of Williams challenging behaviour on others. Williams problems should be private to avoid embarrassment and shame.

Displays of challenging behaviour should be quickly forgotten and the individual with challenging behaviour can move on positively and with hope. Look to the positive and move on, forward!

2) **Take William to a quiet area and talk William through what we are doing**.

Again afford William some privacy and the opportunity and ability to communicate. Give him the tools to tell you what the problem is. After all that's the point of the behaviour and support plan, to understand the individual with challenging behaviour needs and support them.

3) Should the first two strategies fail to diffuse the situation and the display of challenging behaviour continues William

should be left **in a quiet safe room** to be given space for the challenging behaviour to come to a natural end.

4)   **Puzzles and games can be left in the quiet, safe area** to help distract William from his challenging behaviour.

5)   **William can have soothing music** in the quiet, safe area or be allowed to wear headphones.

This change of environment helps William deal with whatever has over challenged. him, and help him manage his behaviour.

Behaviour and support plans are not permanent edifices. They can and indeed must change. The more information on the individual with challenging behaviour you receive the more you understand the individual with challenging behaviour and the more individually tailored the behaviour and support plan can be.

Extra support for the behaviour and support plan to positively support individual with challenging behaviour.

Information is power, the more information you have the better behaviour and support plan you will have. The most common tool for helping you help the individual with challenging behaviour control their challenging behaviour has been discussed previously the ABC chart (Antecedent Behaviour Consequence chart).

This as discussed is a direct observation tool that is used to collect information about events occurring within the individual with challenging behaviour environment.

Although the ABC chart is a common tool of gaining information about an individuals behaviour it is not the most method of gaining information from the individual with challenging behaviour or client.

The most common method is you actually talking to the individual with challenging behaviour before intervening with the complete behaviour and support plan.

Functional assessment

Your initial consultancy, or as it is better known your functional assessment is your first assessments of the individual with challenging behaviour to find answers to an individuals behaviour and the individual themselves. Are there obvious clues from the individuals functional assessment to help them.

Functional assessment helps guide the production of the behaviour and support plan. It helps tailor the behaviour and support plan to the individual. A functional assessment has two possible approaches, both approaches can be used in assessing the individual with challenging behaviour.

1)   **The indirect approaches**

These are questionnaires, interviews, record charts (the ABC chart etc.), reports completed by carers or families of the individual rather than your direct observations.

2)   **The Descriptive approaches**

This method is based on direct observation of the individuals behaviour by the person carrying out the assessment and is done in the natural setting, for example using a chart to record observations of the individuals behaviour at work, at home, at school, on public transport etc.

Answer to Q20: **Explain the importance of person centred approaches in establishing support strategies**.

NHS England states '**It is important that individuals with challenging behaviour should have a person centred care and support plan**".

The person with the most information and the most chance of resolving and managing an individuals behaviour is the individual themselves. That is why it is important to have person centred approaches to establishing your support strategies within your behaviour and support plan.

Support strategies need to be focused on an individuals needs.

What does the individual with challenging behaviour need right now to help them manage their behaviour.

Challenging behaviour is as infinite as the man. It can vary considerably from person to person.

Challenging behaviour can depend on:

1) **The individuals health**.

2) **The individuals background**.

3) **The individuals past experiences**.

4) **Any learning disabilities** etc.

Triggers

Your support strategies should include techniques to manage behaviour that rely on finding the triggers for an individual with challenging behaviours displays, understanding that trigger, and giving them ways to cope with their challenging behaviour.

For example:

1)   An individual who is hypersensitive may need protection from environmental factors such as noise, light, and smells.

2)   An individual who is hypo-sensitive such as a sufferer of autism may need sensory stimulation to stop them banging their heads or hitting or kicking to gain sensory stimulation.

3)   An individual who has been abused in the past may have triggers to displays of challenging behaviour from certain types of people, situations, or places.

Support strategies

As triggers vary from person to person, so are the support strategies. In the past challenging behaviour was often not dealt with in a person centred approach to establish person centred support strategies.

It was usually dealt with by institution centred support strategies with physical restraints, overmedication and containment.

By using a person centred approach you get to know the person rather than know the institution. You begin to understand the reasons for their challenging behaviour.

A person centred plan can be put in place to give the individual a better chance of success. than the old institutionally centred support strategies. Person centred approaches to establishing support strategies increase the ability of the individual with challenging behaviour and therefore increase their quality of life.

Some examples of challenging behaviour and triggers as well as possible person centred support strategies.

John

Behaviour and triggers of John.

John was denied food as a young child and was sometimes left to find food for himself and his baby brother. John has issues with food and often steals food and hides it in his room and clothing and gets into arguments and fights in the dining room.

Support strategies for John.

Johns function of behaviour is quite simple to get food.

From a young age food was very important to John. Although a basic need for survival most people do not have confidence issues over food. But when you are denied this basic component of life either through bad parenting, or lack of funds, food returns to its vital importance.

Without food you will die, you will feel the gnawing of hunger in your belly without guarantee you will eat. In addition Johns food confidence issues are multiplied knowing he has to feed his baby brother too. Johns life focus was getting food all this over many years.

His displays of challenging behaviour all centre around his fear that he will not be able to get food.

Support strategies

1)   **Most important John needs to know there is always enough food for him**.

2)   **Provide John with his own plentiful supply of food in hygienic storage pots in his room.**

3)   **He should not be denied food in the communal rooms.**

Felicity

Behaviours and triggers of Felicity

Felicity has very limited communication skills. Felicity hits other people and kicks and pulls their hair for attention.

Support strategies for Felicity

Felicity's function of behaviour is to get attention through a lack of communication which leads to violent displays of challenging behaviour as she becomes frustrated.

1)   **Felicity feels isolated and left out because she cannot communicate with others and struggles to get attention.**

Felicity needs to be taught alternative communication skills to get attention in the appropriate way.

2)   Felicity should be given a card to let people know she wishes to communicate.

3)   More time and attention should be given to Felicity at the beginning of any activity to allow her to communicate.

4)   Felicity should be taught not to become violent and be rewarded when she shows appropriate behaviour.

Person centred approaches

Person centred approaches are so important to establishing support strategies that many care locations, hospitals, schools, care homes have behaviour support teams specialising in person centred support strategies for individuals with challenging behaviour.

Behaviour Support Teams

Behaviour support teams are set up to support individuals with learning disabilities and their families. They may differ in terms of the services they offer; some may offer assessments for diagnosis or provide different strategies to support individuals with their behaviour. These teams can be made up of a variety of professionals including psychologists, speech and language therapists or medical professionals.

Answer to Q21: Describe how support networks for the individual can help promote positive behaviour.

Support networks promote positive behaviour in individuals with challenging behaviour by including them in activities, and services, and society enabling them to live better and meaningful lives. As evidenced by a 2015 NHS report 'Service Model for Commissioners of Health and Social Services'. Which confirmed that supporting people with autism or learning disabilities that display challenging behaviour promotes positive behaviour when included into a support network.

Types of support networks

1) **Early years service**.

2) **Education** (School and university networks).

3) **Employment** (Support networks from your employer).

4) **Social activities** (Family and carer support networks).

5) **Sports and leisure**.

6) **Training and employment** (Supported internships)

Support and support networks promote positive behaviour by enabling the individual with challenging behaviour to enjoy a better and more meaningful life. It allows the individual with challenging behaviour to promote positive behaviour by allow them:

1) **Access to education.**

2) **Access to employment.**

3) **Access to social activities.**

4) **Access to sports and leisure.**

5) **Access to training.**

6) **The opportunity to develop and maintain good relationships.**

7) **The ability to have as much control and choice over things they do as possible.**

8) **To be empowered to know about the choices available to them.**

Support networks help the individual with challenging behaviour manage their behaviour which means they will be less likely from being excluded from activities, services, opportunities and be more successful in education, employment. Have a more fulfilling social life. All of these results promote positive behaviour in individuals with challenging behaviour.

Support networks are so important in helping promote positive behaviour and improve an individual with challenging behaviour's life that NHS England has stated 'That it is important to support those who display challenging behaviour with support networks" such as:

1)   Specialist multidisciplinary health and social care services working with mainstream services (Behaviour Support Team) like early years, schools, after school clubs, sports clubs, leisure. clubs and employment support.

2)   Social support networks and social activities designed for the individual with challenging behaviour's age group.

NHS England also stated "It was important to have a person centred care and support plan".

Support Networks

What are support networks? Support networks are teams of specialists and professionals who can provide the individual with challenging behaviour with support in many facets of their lives and environments.

1)   **Training the individual with challenging behaviour new skills**.

2)   **Teaching the individual with challenging behaviour new or alternative communication   methods.**

3)   **To provide the individual with challenging behaviour suitable environments**.

4)   To help the individual with challenging behaviour recognise their own limitations and   triggers.

5)   Help the individual with challenging behaviour find ways to avoid displays of   challenging behaviour by finding ways to respond appropriately to triggers.

6)   Assess the individual with challenging behaviour's needs and provide support for the individual with challenging behaviour.

7)   Provide the appropriate and correct level of care.

8)   Help the individual with challenging behaviour make correct and appropriate   decisions.

Answer to Q22: Describe the legislative framework that applies to individuals who present with behaviour that challenges with regard to:

Rights

Human Rights Act 1998

An individual with challenging behaviour has rights just like you and me, and these same rights are protected primarily by the **Human Rights Act 1998**.

In the UK an individual with challenging behaviour's rights are protected by the Human Rights Act 1998. Public authorities such as local authorities, government departments, charities and the NHS must follow this act in everything they do.

The act means that an individual with challenging behaviour has the right to not have their human rights interfered and the above agencies have the responsibility to take positive steps to protect rights when life is endangered or people are being threatened by others.

The act means that the individual with challenging behaviour must have their human rights respected when the above agencies make decisions about them for example where they live and their healthcare.

The Human Rights Act 1998 gives effect or makes legally possible the individual with challenging behaviour's human rights as set out in the European Convention of Human Rights. Because of this human rights are called Convention rights after this important legal event.

An individual with challenging behaviour has the human right or convention right to:

1)   **The right to life.**

2)   **The right to respect for private and family life.**

3)   **The right to freedom of religion and belief as well as other rights.**

An individual with challenging behaviour can take action in the UK court if they feel their human rights have been breached or interfered with.

Safeguarding:

There are a number of laws specific to the safeguarding (**the care and safety**) of the individual with challenging behaviour but the main legislative framework is the Mental Capacity act 2005.

The mental capacity act 2005

The mental capacity act 2005 covers anyone over 16. The act applies to how professionals and other paid carers who work with the individual with challenging behaviour.

The mental capacity act 2005 safeguards the individual with challenging behaviour making it a legal requirement for professional staff and paid carers to follow the guidelines set out in the Mental Capacity Act 2005 code of practice unless there is a good legal reason for not doing so.

The Mental Capacity Act 2005 safeguards the individual with challenging behaviour by aiming to empower and protect people who may not be able to make decisions for themselves.

The Mental Capacity Act 2005 safeguards an individual with challenging behaviour as the acts code of practice enables the individual with challenging behaviour to plan ahead in case they are unable to make important decisions for themselves in the future. **The Mental Capacity Act 2005 and it's code of practice** safeguards an individual with challenging behaviour's choices. The choice they have in their lives and what choices they have for the future should they lose the capability to make such decisions.

The Mental Capacity Act 2005 and it's code of practice ensures the individual with challenging behaviour has:

1) The decision of where to live.

2) The decision of who to live with.

3) The decision of choice of medical treatment.

4) The decision of choice of healthcare.

5) The decision of choice of management of personal finances.

6) The decision of choice of social care provision.

7) The decision of choice carer.

8) The decision of choice whether to enter to enter a personal relationship.

9) The decision of of choice of what they want to wear.

10) The decision of choice of what they want to eat.

11) The decision of which activities they want to take part in.

12) The decision of whether to let staff help with personal care like washing and bathing.

13) The decision of whether to spend time outside.

14) The decision of whether to stay out late.

15) **The decision of whether to go on a trip or holiday**.

16) **The decision of whether to go shopping**.

The mental capacity act 2005

The Mental Capacity Act 2005 and it's code of practice dovetails with the Human Rights Act of 1998 to allow the rights of an individual with challenging behaviour to be protected as far as is legally possible should an individual with challenging behaviour lose the capacity to make major and day to day decisions regarding their lives. It is designed to safeguard the individual with challenging behaviour should it get to a point the individual is beyond the capacity to make decisions for themselves.

Safeguards of the Mental Capacity act 2005 and its Code of Practice

The Mental Capacity Act 2005 and it's code of practice works on the principle that everyone is assumed to have the capacity to make decisions for themselves if they are given enough information, support, and time. It's aim is to protect (safeguard) the rights to make their own decisions and be involved in any decisions that affect them.

The Mental Capacity Act 2005 and its code of practice is a legislative framework that safeguards the individual with challenging behaviour by ensuring that **an individual with challenging behaviour's capacity is judged according to specific decisions that have to be made according to the act and not just the illness or condition they have. A person centred approach rather than an institutional based approach.**

The Mental Capacity Act 2005 and it's code of practice ensure an individuals capacity to make their own decisions are not judged on their illness, disability, age, appearance or behaviour. Regardless of an individuals challenging behaviour their capacity to make decisions is not based on their challenging behaviour. Their capacity to make decisions is legally safeguarded by the Mental Capacity Act 2005 and it's code of practice. **The Act must be followed when making a decision on behalf of an individual with challenging behaviour who legally lacks the capacity to make decisions.** Also the Mental Capacity Act 2005 and it's code of practice requires that all such decisions be made **in the best interest of the individual with challenging behaviour.**

The Mental Health Act 2007

The Mental Health Act 2007 provides safeguards to patients to ensure they are not inappropriately treated, under the provisions of the Mental Health Act 2007.

Safeguarding Vulnerable Groups Act 2006

Another important legislative framework that applies to the safeguarding of individuals who present with challenging behaviour is the Safeguarding Vulnerable Groups Act 2006.

The safeguarding of Vulnerable Groups Act 2006 was created following the Bichard Inquiry Recommendations. The Safeguarding of Vulnerable Groups Act 2006 came into force and introduced the Independent Safeguarding Authority (ISA) which alongside the responsibilities of vetting and monitoring appropriate individuals, maintains the Adults Barred List and the Children's Barred List.

These lists safeguard individuals with challenging behaviour by identifying those not permitted to work in a regulated activity with vulnerable adults and/or children.

The Safeguarding of Vulnerable Groups Act 2006 safeguards the individual with challenging behaviour by promoting safe recruitment.

Safe Recruitment

In 2010 a review of criminal records, disclosure and barring systems was undertaken by the government. This review resulted in the Disclosure and Barring Services (DBS) being formed which took over the functions of the Criminal Records Bureau (CRB) and the Independent Safeguarding Authority (ISA) in 2012.

Due to the Safeguarding of Vulnerable Groups Act 2006 it is an offence under the law for an organisation to knowingly appoint someone in a regulated activity who has been barred from working with a vulnerable group. Likewise it is an offence under the law for someone barred by the Disclosure and Barring Service to work with vulnerable groups.

It is a legal requirement that anyone perceived as having caused harm to an individual with challenging behaviour or will cause harm to an individual with challenging behaviour be referred to the Disclosure and Barring Service.

Deprivation of Liberty

The Mental Health Act 2007

The Mental Health Act 2007 provides safeguards to patients to ensure they are not inappropriately treated, under the provisions of the Mental Health Act 2007.

The Human Rights Act 1998, and the Mental Capacity Act 2005 cover certain acts of deprivation of liberty under the law, but the Mental Health Act 2007 is the main legislative framework regarding to the legality of an individual with challenging behaviour being deprived of their liberty.

The Mental Health Act 2007 is designed to give health professionals the legal power under certain circumstances to detain, assess, and treat people with mental disorders in the interests of their health and safety and the public's health and safety.

In effect if the individual with challenging behaviour puts themselves or others at risk, they can be deprived of their liberty, assess against their will and have to accept treatment they do not want.

Although this goes against the Human Rights Act 1998 and the Mental Capacity Act 2005, it is legally allowed and necessary since it is in the individual with challenging behaviour's best interest to their health and safety and the health and safety of those around them and the public in general.

In a contest of rights under the law, the rights of the general public outweigh individual rights.

Mental Health Act 1983

The 1983 Mental Health Act laid down provisions for the deprivation of liberty for an individual with challenging behaviour. In the Mental Health Act 1983 there are provisions laid down for the compulsory detention and treatment of people with mental health problems in England and Wales.
The Mental health act amends and extends the powers of compulsion and introduces compulsory community treatment orders.

Compulsory Community Treatment Orders

A Compulsory Community Treatment Order is a legal order that makes a patient compliant with an ordered treatment. Legal treatment becomes a legal statutory requirement if so ordered through the Mental Health Act 1983 and the Mental Health Act 2007. Therefore both acts can cause an individual with challenging behaviour of their liberty.

The 2007 Mental Health Act also focuses on public protection and risk management.

Essentially if the Mental Capacity Act 2005 is a legal shield that favours the individual with challenging behaviour the Mental Health Acts 1983 and 2007 are legal shields that favours the public.

The Mental Health Acts deals with the Deprivation of Liberty by making it a legal requirement that to be forcibly admitted for assessment, the admission **must be authorised by two section 12 doctors and an approved mental health professional, who both have to agree that**:

A)   **The patient is suffering from a mental disorder of a nature or degree that warrants detention in hospital for assessment.**

B)   **The patient ought to be detained for his or her own health or safety, or the protection of others.**

The Mental Health Act 2007 also covers the **admission for assessment in emergency cases** and **admission for treatment, detention and the power of the police to remove individuals from a public place, if they need to be taken to a place of safety or require immediate care and control.**

The Mental Health Act 2007 also introduced **deprivation of liberty safeguards** by **amending the Mental Health Act 2005.** As well as also **extending the rights of victims of crime by amending the Domestic Violence, Crime and Victims Act 2004.**

The Domestic Violence, Crime and Victims Act 2004

The Domestic Violence, Crime and Victims Act 2004 extended safeguards and gives extra protection against deprivation of liberty through various amendments.

Deprivation of Liberty Safeguards (DoLs)

Within the legislative framework are the **deprivation of liberty safeguards** which come into force in England and Wales in 2009 **under amendments of the Mental Capacity Act 2005.**

Since there are many individuals with challenging behaviour in different settings who are deprived of their liberty due to the treatment they receive or the level of restriction they are subject to. **Especially in institutionally centred environments.**

Individuals with challenging behaviour can find themselves **unable to consent** because **they lack the mental capacity to do so**. Dementia patients are a good example of this.

The amendments to the Mental Capacity Act 2005 produced the **Deprivation of Liberty Safeguards (DoLs)** which relates to people who are placed in social care settings such as care homes or hospitals for their care or treatment and who lack mental capacity.

The Deprivation of Liberty Safeguards was introduced when the **European Court of Human Rights (ECHR)** found that English Law (Mental Capacity Act 2005, and the Mental Health Acts) did not give adequate protection to the individual with challenging behaviour who lacked the mental capacity to **'consent to care'** or **'consent to medical treatment'** and **whose behaviour or condition needed limits put upon their liberty to keep them and others safe**.

The Deprivation of Liberty Safeguards are part of wide legislation designed to protect the rights of the individual with challenging behaviour who lack the mental capacity to 'consent to care' or 'consent to medical treatment'. The Deprivation of Liberty Safeguards also link more fully into the Human Rights Act 1998 and it's Commission Rights.

Deprivation of Liberty Safeguards is intended to:

1)   **Protect people who lack the mental capacity from being detained when this is not in their best interests.**

2)   **Prevent arbitrary detention.**

3)   **Give people the rights to challenge decisions.**

The difference between deprivation of liberty and restriction of liberty

The law's aim and the legislative frameworks aim is to make **a legal division between 'deprivation of liberty' (which is illegal) and 'restriction of liberty' (which is medically legal).**

The legal difference between deprivation of liberty and restriction of liberty is one of 'degree' or 'intensity'. The law and general practice envisages a scale that moves from 'restraint' or 'restriction' to 'deprivation of liberty'. This code of practice includes a list of factors that have to be legally taken into account as ordered by the European Court of Human Rights via the Human Rights Act 1998 and the amendments to the Mental Capacity Act 2005 known as the Deprivation of Liberty Safeguards.

Legal factors in determining deprivation of liberty

1) **The amount, and type of restraint used (the legal 'degree' of the restraint being used) I.e. is the individual with challenging behaviour sedated, by 'what' and 'how much'. What is the reason for the restraint, and how long is the individual with challenging behaviour restrained.**

2) **The degree staff exercises complete and effective control over the care and movement of an individual with challenging behaviour for a significant period**.

3) **The degree staff exercise control over assessments, treatments, contacts and residence**.

4) **If a decision taken by the institution that the individual with challenging behaviour will not be released**

into the care of others, or permitted to live elsewhere, unless the staff in the institution consider it appropriate.

5)   A request by the carers for an individual with challenging behaviour to be discharged to their care is refused.

6)   The individual with challenging behaviour is unable to maintain social contacts because of restrictions placed on their access to other people.

7)   The individual with challenging behaviour loses autonomy because they are under continuous supervision and control.

Legally these factors are not conclusive on there own and would have to be considered in each individual case and be dependent on circumstance but given enough degree or intensity these factors legally determine if an individual with challenging behaviour is being legally restrained in their best interests or being illegally deprived of their liberty. The law will ask you are you the individual with challenging behaviour's carer or their kidnapper.

Deprivation of Liberty Safeguards in action

Due to the amendments to the Mental Capacity Act 2005 which resulted in the Deprivation of Liberty Safeguards. The Supreme Court handed down judgements in two specific cases in March 2014, **Cheshire West and Chester Council** and **Surrey Council** (P&Q vs Council). The judgements commonly known as **'Cheshire West'** led to a **considerable increase in the number of individuals with challenging behaviour in England and Wales being legally considered deprived of their liberty for the purposes of receiving care and treatment.**

The judgement emphasised the importance of identifying those who are deprived of their liberty so that their circumstances can be the subject of regular independent checks to ensure that decisions being made about them are actually made in their best interests. Power corrupts and absolute power corrupts absolutely.

The Care Act 2014

It is not just individuals with challenging behaviour that have rights and legislative frameworks that protect and safeguard those rights. Carers have rights too and legislative frameworks to protect them. Like individuals with challenging behaviour, carers have the Human Rights Act 1998 but carers also have the Care Act 2014. The Care Act which came into force April 2015, outlines a carers legal rights to assessment and support.

Under the Care Act 2014 a carer is anyone who supports an individual with challenging behaviour such as a friend or a relative, not a professional carer or somebody who works in a voluntary organisation.

If you have a personal or family connection to an individual with challenging behaviour and are their carer you are covered by this act. If you don't have a personal connection to the individual with challenging behaviour or are a paid professional you are not covered by this act.

The Care Act 2014 is primarily aimed at carers who are the friends and family of the individual with challenging behaviour. Prior to the Care Act 2014 such personal carers did not have the legal right of support.

There was no legal recognition that the care by friends and family of the individual with challenging behaviour was hard work and that the carers themselves would be challenged. Also any support received by the carer was at the discretion of the local authority. This meant before the Care Act 2014 there was no legal right to access any support whatsoever.

The support you would receive as a personal carer varied upon such things as the area you were in and the resources given by the local authority. The act focuses on personal carers eighteen and over.

The Care Act 2014

1)   **Allows family circumstances to be considered when making an assessment of an adults care needs.**

2)   **Rules are provided under the act so that carers of disabled children are provided with planned transition into adult care and support.**

3)   **Before the Care Act 2014 the carer had to provide a substantial amount of care on a regular basis to qualify for an assessment of support.**

In other words you had to be the main carer doing a substantial amount of care for the individual with challenging behaviour before a local authority would even legally need to see you let alone need to offer you any support.

The Care Act 2014 now makes it the legal responsibility of local councils to assess a cares need for support. The Care Act 2014 means more carers are able to receive an assessment which considers the impact of caring on the carer.

Legal guidance under the Care Act 2014 provides on how carers are supported once the best way to meet their needs is assessed.

The planning process in assessing the needs of a carer legally involves:

1) **The local authority.**

2) **The individuals with challenging behaviour you are caring for.**

3) **The carer themselves.**

4) **Any person the carer wishes to be involved like their solicitor etc.**

Answer to Question 23: **Describe agreed ways of working to protect an individual who presents with behaviour that challenges.**

What are agreed way? **Agreed ways are agreed ways of working which are established within the policies and procedures in formal documentation within the workplace.** It is important to adhere to the agreed scope of your job role as this defines the role and responsibilities which you are expected to meet.

Agreed ways established within your workplaces policies and procedures protect an individual who presents with behaviour that challenges by making sure professional staff adhere to their professional roles and have their roles and responsibilities defined. This means that professional staff should not work outside their job role and must work within it.

By working outside your role or failure to adhere to agreed ways within your workplace's policies and procedures you can:

1)   Put yourself, the individual with challenging behaviour, colleges and employers at risk of needs and expectations not being met.

2)   Leave yourself and others open to harm and injury or prosecution or to the suggestion (legal risk) of failing to meet the appropriate standards required.

To protect individuals who present behaviour that challenges and provide the right support it is important to follow the agreed ways of working.

The Agreed Ways of Working include:

1)   Providing appropriate care for service users in line with organisational polices and   procedures.

2)   Managing/organising and updating information for individuals at each point of contact   and recording in appropriate documentation.

3)   Communicating and providing information by relevant methods internally and   externally, in accordance with organisational polices and procedures.

4)   Supporting independent individuals to maintain their independence for as long as   possible and communicate all changes with relevant persons.

5)   Adhere to health and safety within the workplace in relation to roles and response and in accordance with organisational polices and procedures.

6)   Undertake training and regular continuing professional development (CPD) in line   with organisational polices and procedures.

There are further agreed ways of working with regard to health and safety within a care setting.

1)   **Using systems correctly.**

2)   **Reporting of incidents.**

3)   **Moving and handling.**

4)   **Safe use of equipment.**

5)   **Slips, trips and falls on a level.**

6)   **Falls from height**

7)   **Hazardous substances, infections and diseases.**

8)   **Hot water and hot surfaces.**

9)   **Work related violence and aggression.**

10)   **Working environment**

11)   **General welfare.**

The agreed ways of working to protect an individual who presents with behaviour that challenges is further extended and enforced by the Mental Health Act 2007. The Mental Health Act 2007 provides legal guidance to health professionals on how they should proceed when undertaking duties under the act.

The guiding principles of the Mental Health Act 2007 which should be considered are:

1)   Decisions must be taken with a view to maximising the safety and well-being of the   individual who presents with behaviour that challenges.

2)   Promoting the recovery of the individual with challenging behaviour and protecting   others from harm.

3)   Minimise the restrictions placed upon the individual who presents with challenging   behaviour's liberty.

4)   Respect the individual who presents with challenging behaviour's past and present   wishes and feelings, taking into account diversity in religion, culture and sexual orientation.

5)   Involve the individual who presents with challenging behaviour in planning,   developing and delivering their care and treatment.

6)   Ensure effective and efficient use of resources.

General Principles of Care

Some of the agreed ways of working that protects an individual who presents with challenging behaviour are **the General Principles of Care**.

The National Institute for Health and Care Excellence (NICE) has produced principles of care. These principles of care are enforced when working with individuals with a learning disability and behaviour that challenges and their families and carers.

General Principles of Care require that support and interventions take into account **the severity of the persons learning disability, their development stage** and **any communication difficulties** or **physical or mental health problems**.

The General Principles of Care state that support and interventions provided should:

1) **Take place in the least restrictive setting as possible, such as the individual who presents with challenging behaviour home or as close to the home environment as possible.**

2) **Be available in other places where the individual who presents with challenging behaviour regularly spends time such as school or residential care.**

3) **Aim to prevent, reduce or stop the development of future episodes of behaviour that challenges.**

4) **Aim to improve the quality of life.**

5) **Offer support and interventions respectfully.**

6) **Ensure that the focus is on improving the individuals support and increasing their skills rather than changing the individual.**

7) **Offer a second opinion if required.**

8) **Offer independent advocacy to the person and to their family members or carers.**

A final agreed way of working to protect an individual who presents with challenging behaviour is the agrees way of letting your boss or organisation know there is a problem or a contravention of the General Principles of Care, Mental Health Act 2005, Mental Health Act 2009, the Deprivation of Liberty Safeguards, the Mental Capacity Act 2005, or the Human Rights Act 1998. Employer's should provide or explain these whistle blowing policies to employees.

In a health and social setting you have the responsibility to report things that you feel are wrong or illegal or if anyone is neglecting their duties. The wrongdoing or contravention disclosed must be in the public interest and if this the case the 'whistle blower' is protected by the law as long as the complaint falls into one of the following categories:

1) **A miscarriage of justice.**

2) **A criminal offense.**

3) **A risk or damage to the environment.**

4) **Someone's health and safety being in danger.**

5) **The organisation breaking the law.**

6) **A belief someone is covering up an inappropriate practice.**

Answer to Question 24: Describe how to monitor interventions and safeguard individuals

Monitoring interventions

Monitoring interventions is important and necessary. **Monitoring interventions enables you to monitor how effective the interventions have been and what can be done in the future**. The most common way of monitoring interventions is through record keeping especially through a behaviour support plan.

There are many ways to safeguard individuals in your care. Bearing in mind the Human Rights Act 1998, the Mental Capacity Act 2005, the Mental Health Act 2007, the Deprivation of Liberty Safeguards, the Care Act 2014, the Safeguarding of Vulnerable groups Act, 2006, the agreed ways of working within your organisation and the Guiding Principles of Care (as produced by NICE) and your own common sense and humanity.

Ways to protect individuals that present with challenging behaviour through the above:

1)   **You must safeguard an individuals health and well-being**.

2)   **You must safeguard an individuals human rights**.

3)   **You must protect their right to live free form harm, abuse and neglect**.

4)   **You must safeguard individuals from maltreatment or things that are bad for your health**.

5) **You must provide circumstances that allows safe and effective care**.

6) **You must make sure individuals are not at risk from neglect**.

7) **Take into account their views, feelings, beliefs, and wishes**.

The way to do this is to follow the acts, principles and recommendations of the legal acts, General Principles of Care and agreed ways (**policies and procedures**) of your organisation.

You may also inform the **Care Quality Commission** if you have any concerns regarding your company or the quality of the individuals care.

Care Quality Commission

The Care Quality Commission (CQC) safeguards individuals in health and social care settings by:

1) **Using information received to look at the risks to people who use care services**.

2) **Refer concerns to local councils and/or the police for further investigation**.

3) **Carry out inspections to help identify safeguarding concerns**.

4) **Publish findings on safeguarding in inspection reports**.

5)   **Taking actions if care services don't have suitable arrangements to keep people safe.**

6)   **Working with partners such as the police, local councils, health agencies, other   regulators, and government departments.**

7)   **Taking part in multi-agency children's safeguarding inspections.**

To get a picture of children's and young people's experiences and how well they are being safeguarded.

Recording and monitoring incidents of challenging behaviour and the possible triggers is a great way of safeguarding individuals. Since accurate and effective documentation and monitoring can help reduce incidents of challenging behaviour, deal with situations in the bet way possible when they do occur and ensure safeguarding issues are managed.

What your behaviour support plans and monitoring interventions and safeguarding documentation should do is help you identify patterns to predict when challenging behaviour is more likely to occur. This helps with planning properly and preventing challenging behaviour.

Thank you very much in taking the time to review my work.

Pedro Ramalho

Printed in Great Britain
by Amazon

46080360R00095